Contents

PART III
Teacher Professionalism and Teacher Education

PART IV
Teaching

The Teaching for Social Justice Series

Teaching the Personal and the Political

Essays on Hope and Justice

WILLIAM AYERS

TEACHERS
COLLEGE
PRESS
Teachers College, Columbia University
New York and London

The author and publisher are grateful for permission to reprint excerpts from the following:

"Still I Rise", copyright © 1978 by Maya Angelou, from *And Still I Rise* by Maya Angelou. Used by permission of Random House, Inc. (U.S. and world rights)

"Consider Me" from *The Collected Poems of Langston Hughes* by Langston Hughes, copyright © 1994 by the estate of Langston Hughes. Used by permission of Alfred A. Knopf, a division of Random House, Inc. (U.S. and world rights)

"To Be of Use" from *Circles on the Water* by Marge Piercy, copyright © 1982 by Marge Piercy. Used by permission of Alfred A. Knopf, a division of Random House, Inc. (U.S. and world rights)

"To be of Use" by Marge Piercy, copyright © 1973, 1982 by Marge Piercy and Middlemarsh, Inc. From *Circles On The Water,* Alfred A. Knopf. 1982. (U.K. rights)

"The Poets Obligation" from *Fully Empowered* by Pablo Neruda, translated by Alastair Reid. Translation copyright © 1975 by Alastair Reid. Reprinted by permission of Farrar, Straus and Giroux, LLC.

"To The Bone" by Tahar Ben Jelloun. Copyright © 1999 *Racism Explained to My Daughter* by Tahar Ben Jelloun. Reprinted by permission of The New Press. (800) 233-4830

The author and publisher are grateful for permission to reprint chapters that originally appeared elsewhere:

Chapter 2: Ayers, William, *Journal for a Just and Caring Education, 2*(1), pp. 85–92, copyright © 2003 by Corwin Press. Reprinted by permission of Corwin Press, Inc.

Chapter 5: Originally published in *Democracy and Education*, Volume 7, No. 2, published by the Institute for Democracy in Education.

Chapter 6: First printed in the *Heartland Journal*. Reprinted by permission.

Chapter 13: Ayers, William, *Journal of Teacher Education, 34*(5), pp. 24–31. copyright © 1988 by Corwin Press. Reprinted by permission of Corwin Press, Inc.

Chapter 19: *Empowering Teachers and Parents*, G. A. Hess, Jr. Copyright © 1992 by Greenwood Publishing Group, Inc. Reprinted with permission of Greenwood Publishing Group, Inc., Westport, CT.

Published by Teachers College Press, 1234 Amsterdam Avenue, New York, NY 10027

Copyright © 2004 by Teachers College, Columbia University

Library of Congress Cataloging-in-Publication Data

Ayers, William, 1944–
    Teaching the personal and the political : essays on hope and justice / William Ayers.
      p. cm. — (The teaching for social justice series)
    Includes bibliographic references and index.
    ISBN 0-8077-4461-1 (cloth : alk. paper) — ISBN 0-8077-4460-3 (pbk. : alk. paper)
    1. Critical pedagogy—United States. 2. Social justice—Study and teaching—United States. 3. Teachers—Professional relationships—United States. I. Title. II. Series.

LC196.5.U6A94   2004
370.11'5—dc22   2003068739

ISBN 0-8077-4460-3 (paper)
ISBN 0-8077-4461-1 (cloth)

Printed on acid-free paper
Manufactured in the United States of America

11 10 09 08 07 06 05 04   8 7 6 5 4 3 2 1

Preface

These essays, written over a period of about 15 years, are a chronicle of a particular obsession that has held me for most of my adult life. They are, as well, a direct result of living in the heart of Chicago, and of working at the University of Illinois at Chicago, a sprawling university in the heart of America's singular modern city.

First, the obsession.

I came to teaching when I was 20 years old. I visited a friend's classroom where a group of happy youngsters embraced me and drew me into their play, an enchanted world of their own creation. From that time onward, I've been captivated by teaching, and have recognized it as a fundamentally relational activity, an enterprise driven by human connection, emotion, and imagination, one characterized by involvement and affinity, attraction and sympathy. It achieves, at its best, a unique kind of intimacy.

I began teaching in a preschool affiliated with the Civil Rights Movement, a tiny independent precursor to Head Start. Since then, teaching has been linked for me to basic moral concerns about rightness and fairness, punctuated with phrases like, "Use your words," "That hurts her feelings," "Let's all try to be fair," and "You can't say you can't play."

In fact, I walked out of a jail cell and directly into my first teaching job. I'd been arrested during a sit-in, and learned about an insurgent little free school from a fellow activist; I surprised myself by being intrigued enough to go straight for a visit. I never looked back. For me, teaching has always been an undertaking whose basic structure, root and branch, gestures toward social justice, inviting people to reach, to stretch, to change their lives, and to change the world. The cornerstone of teaching is a kind of truth-in-action.

After a few years of teaching followed by some time off, I returned to work in the preschool my oldest child had just begun attending. As it happens, for several years in that school I was the teacher to all three of our children. Ever since, I've known teaching as achingly personal, always improvisational, grounded in acts of attention and witness, powered by hope and faith.

These linked stories of how I was taken by teaching—each true, and yet each offering an altered angle of regard, each emphasizing a slightly different edge—underline a fundamental fact: all human beings live storied lives. As Muriel Rukeyser so elegantly puts it, "the universe is made up of stories, not atoms." Each teacher and each student narrates a life. Some narratives are overdramatized, some melodramatic—they can be tragic or funny, soap opera or high opera—but it is through our narratives that we develop and negotiate an identity. The stories we tell ourselves can mystify and confuse us, or they can open us, propel forward motion to more intentional choices and more powerful conclusions. Our stories are dynamic and in-motion, always changing with new conditions, and always suggesting alternative outcomes. The stories I know of teaching, the ones I tell and retell, are mostly invitations to an ideal, to teaching as ethical action. They are stories in which we recognize the great humanizing mission of education, the foundational core of the enterprise: teaching as a commitment to enlightenment and liberation. This has been my passion and my obsession.

*   *   *

I didn't set out 15 years ago to write essays; I'd written almost nothing before, and hadn't thought much about the art of the essay. But personal essays are largely what I've done. I've come to admire the form, discovering that in many ways it suits my temperament, my interests, and my particular subject—my obsession with teaching. There's a freedom in the essay, a license to expand horizons and cross the boundaries so fiercely guarded in the balkanized fiefdoms of the Academy. The personal essay inspires voyages. It suggests a space to experiment; it invites skepticism, agnosticism, even subversion.

Just as teachers create environments for students that are pregnant with possibilities for discovery, they must build and nourish those surroundings and contexts for themselves. When teachers write about teaching—capacious, mysterious, immeasurable—the essay is a perfect match. Since thought and reflection can be provoked by anything, and wisdom radiates from various and surprising places, popping up at unpredictable moments, the trick is to be ready. An overheard conversation on a bus, the odd line in the morning paper, a thought from a letter, scenes from a film—each can be the occasion for insight, challenge, a change in direction. This method— call it mindful serendipity—may not be the most efficient nor the most useful for sustained study, but it has served my purposes, enabling me to explore something both venerable and ineffable.

*   *   *

I came to the University of Illinois at Chicago as an assistant professor in the fall of 1987, fresh out of graduate school with a newly-minted doctorate from Teachers College, Columbia University. In the spring of that year, moments after I had defended my dissertation, six-year-old Malik said, "So Poppy, you're a doctor, right?— but not the kind who can help anybody." Right, I agreed. But he was only partly right. Teachers can't necessarily fix bodies. But—as I argue in many of the essays collected here—if teachers fulfill their moral obligation, they can in fact help a student to answer the question, "Who am I in this world?"

In any case, UIC proved to be precisely the right place at exactly the right time for me. In the grand tradition, it is a place devoted to free inquiry and free thought, to open, often rough-and-tumble dialogue, and to accomplishment and intellectual productivity rather than clout and connection. It is a big, shambling, urban university suffering, for both good and bad, an adolescent temperament—uncertain one minute and all-too-certain the next, insecure and arrogant, striving, energetic, out-of-control, turbulent. Eager to be seen as a grown-up, UIC's identity is in constant flux, and its eagerness betrays the dynamic and conflicted state it inhabits. UIC is unsettled and unsettling, and teaching there is both learned and practiced on-the-run. Teaching helps students find their place in the world, and UIC has helped me locate my place as an educator as well.

UIC is filled with luminous pockets of excellence, with students and teachers who are brilliant, serious, thoughtful, and committed. Its publicness is its defining feature: my students are often first-generation in college, my graduate students the first in their families to get an advanced degree. To take one revealing example: a couple of years ago I spoke to the Honors College students and their families before Commencement. It was, as these occasions tend to be, moving and meaningful, especially for parents and loved ones. The next day I was giving a talk at the School of Law at Northwestern University, a private school on the North Shore. I arrived early to check out the room, and the custodian setting up the chairs looked up, smiled, and said hello. "I heard you speak yesterday," he said. "My daughter graduated with honors from UIC."

UIC, like the city it grew up in, is tempestuous, fresh, and excited, a place of creative tension and productive conflict. Chicago, still the city of big shoulders, still the windy city, still the home of the blues, is the *Jungle* in one account, *American Apartheid* in another. It's Richard Wright, Gwendolyn Brooks, and Studs Terkel; *City on the Make* and city by the lake. This, too, has suited me. This quintessentially American city has been my classroom from the start, its influences on my thinking and my work inestimable. These essays reflect, I think, the dialectic of the place in which they were created.

Teaching the Personal and the Political

Essays on Hope and Justice

CHAPTER 1

Introduction:
Teaching as an Ethical Enterprise

These essays arise out of a lifelong passion for teaching, and a pre-occupation with both its possibilities and its discontents. I began teaching in 1965 in a small free school—one free of traditional, publically mandated requirements—associated with the civil rights movement, and from that moment until now teaching has been linked for me with the idea of a quest—the hope someone may harbor for a better life, the movement of individuals and of whole peoples toward enlightenment and freedom, the flash of imaginations as a fairer and more decent world comes into clearer focus. In every classroom I've been in since—from preschool to graduate school, from the community center to the detention center, in both the tony and the tough parts of town—I've tried to take as my beacon, my guide, this primal sense that teaching at its best urges voyages, that teaching can be both life-altering and world-changing.

This orientation necessarily sends me on my own voyages, explorations of my students' lives as well as my own, and expeditions into the concentric circles of context—cultural surroundings, historical flow, economic condition—within which each of us lives and works. The inexhaustible liveliness of teaching can be found here, for the world never stands still, and neither do her people.

All human beings, and most propulsively our children, are wiggly, squirming, luminous, impatient, in motion; each is an unruly spark of meaning-making energy, dashing from here to there in the blink of an eye. Each, as one kindergarten teacher once said, arrives at school as a bold exclamation point and a bright question mark; we should do our best to resist turning them into dull periods after only a few years of schooling.

One of my early mentors was Myles Horton, founder of the

Highlander Folk School in Tennessee, a school that taught the activists who would later lead the assault on segregation in the South. Myles believed that the people with the problems are also the experts on solving those problems. Like Paulo Freire, Myles opposed the notion that teaching involves making small deposits into inert little banks. His pedagogy began with people coming together to name their problems and to collectively seek and organize the solutions. The content arose from the participants themselves, and solutions were sought through dialogue and reflective action. Myles believed that the purpose of education was to participate in correcting unfair privilege and unfair deprivation—education, he said, must take account of the needs of the existing community life, and it must proceed with the intention of improving the life we live in common.

This essential, central truth of teaching is often overlooked, usually missed by teachers themselves, almost always by the larger public. My wife is a lawyer, and for years I've found myself, often a bit incongruously, at lawyer parties. The casual chitchat follows a familiar rhythm:

> *Lawyer:* What do you do?
> *Me:* I teach kindergarten (or in another year—"I teach in the juvenile detention center").
> *Lawyer:* (Invariably moving on with a patronizing, pitying look) Oh . . . That must be interesting.

After a while I tired of the whole predictable script, and developed what I thought was a snappier response. The dialogue now went like this:

> *Lawyer:* What do you do?
> *Me:* I teach kindergarten . . . It's the most intellectually demanding thing I've ever done.

This invariably causes a head snap as the lawyer tries to reconcile three words: *teach, kindergarten, intellectual.* But the effect is short-lived.

> *Lawyer:* (Recomposing the pitying look) That must be *very, very* interesting.

Reaching for an even grander rejoinder, I try this:

Lawyer: What do you do?
Me: I teach kindergarten, the most intellectually demanding thing I've ever done, and if you ever are bored with reading the warranties on appliances and making six figures, and you decide to do something useful with your life, you ought to give it a try . . .

I seldom get that far and rarely pique enough interest for another round. The lawyer moves on, the words crash to the floor, and I am left feeling naive, reprimanded, adrift in an indifferent world with my pathetic little dreams of teaching. But I'm not entirely wrong to try. So in what way is teaching intellectual work? How is teaching an ethical enterprise?

A primary challenge to teachers is to see each student as a three-dimensional creature, a person much like themselves, with hopes, dreams, aspirations, skills, and capacities; with a body and a mind and a heart and a spirit; with experience, history, a past, several possible pathways, a future. This knotty, complicated challenge requires patience, curiosity, wonder, awe, humility. It demands sustained focus, intelligent judgment, inquiry and investigation. It requires wide-awakeness, since every judgment is contingent, every view partial, every conclusion tentative. The student is dynamic, alive, and forever in motion. Nothing is settled once and for all. No view is all views and no perspective every perspective. The student grows and changes—yesterday's need is forgotten, today's claim is all-encompassing and brand-new. This, then, is an intellectual task of serious and huge proportion.

As difficult as this challenge is, it is made tougher and more intense because teachers typically work in schools, institutions of hierarchy and power, command and control, where the toxic habit of labeling kids by their deficits has achieved the power of common sense. The language of schools is a language of labeling, a language of reduction, a language lacking spark, dynamism, imagination. TAG, LD, BD, EMH, FBT—whatever these point to, even when glimpsing a chunk of reality, is reduced and overdetermined in schools. The thinking teacher needs to look beneath and beyond the labels.

Another basic challenge to teachers is to stay wide awake to the world, to the concentric circles of context in which we live and work. Teachers must know and care about aspects of our shared life—our calling is to shepherd and enable the callings of others. Teachers, then, invite students to become somehow more capable, more thoughtful and powerful in their choices, more engaged in a culture and a civilization. How do we warrant that invitation? How do we understand this culture and civilization?

Teachers choose—they choose how to see the world, what to embrace and what to reject, whether to support or resist this or that directive. As teachers choose, the ethical emerges. James Baldwin (1988) says:

> The paradox of education is precisely this—that as one begins to become conscious one begins to examine the society in which he is being educated. The purpose of education, finally, is to create in a person the ability to look at the world for himself, to make his own decisions, to say to himself this is black or this is white, to decide for himself whether there is a God in heaven or not. To ask questions of the universe, and then learn to live with those questions, is the way he achieves his own identity. But no society is really anxious to have that kind of person around. What societies really, ideally, want is a citizenry which will simply obey the rules of society. If a society succeeds in this, that society is about to perish. The obligation of anyone who thinks of himself as responsible is to examine society and try to change it and to fight it—at no matter what risk. This is the only hope society has. This is the only way societies change (p. 4).

Teachers can become the midwives of hope, but in another register they can be the purveyors of determinism and despair. Here, for example, we discover in literature quite different teachers at work:

In *Beloved,* Toni Morrison's (2000) searing novel of slavery, freedom, and the complexities of a mother's love, School Teacher, a frightening character with no other name, comes to Sweet Home with his efficient, scientific interest in slaves and makes life unbearable for the people there. School Teacher is a disturbing, jarring character for those of us who want to think of teachers as caring and compassionate people. School Teacher is cold, sadistic, and brutal— the master of control and management, champion of the status quo. He and others like him are significant props in an entire system of dehumanization, oppression, and exploitation. When the young girl

Denver wonders aloud if she might go to school, to Oberlin College, a place that represents to her the possibility of opening to a wider world, of moving beyond what she has always known, an older character, thinks to himself that there is nothing in the world more dangerous than a white schoolteacher.

Toward the end of Amir Maalouf's dazzling *Samarkand*, a historical novel of the life of Omar Khayyám and the journey of the *Rubáiyát*, Howard Baskerville, a British schoolteacher in the city of Tabriz in old Persia at the time of the first democratic revolution, explains an incident in which he was observed weeping in the marketplace: "Crying is not a recipe for anything," he begins, "Nor is it a skill. It is simply a naked, naive and pathetic gesture" (Maalouf, 1994, p. 234). But, he goes on, crying is nonetheless important. When the people saw him crying they figured that he "had thrown off the sovereign indifference of a foreigner," and at that moment they could come to Baskerville "to tell me confidentially that crying serves no purpose and that Persia does not need any extra mourners and that the best I could do would be to provide the children of Tabriz with an adequate education." "If they had not seen me crying," Baskerville concludes, "they would never have let me tell the pupils that this Shah was rotten and that the religious chiefs of Tabriz were hardly any better" (p. 234).

Both teachers show us that teaching occurs in context, and that pedagogy and technique are not the wellsprings of moral choice. Teaching becomes ethical practice when it is guided by an unshakable commitment to helping human beings reach the full measure of their humanity, and a willingness to reach toward a future fit for all—a place of peace and justice.

In *A Lesson Before Dying*, Ernest Gaines (1993) creates a riveting portrait of a teacher locked in struggle with a resistant student, wrestling as well with his own doubts and fears about himself as a teacher and a person, and straining against the outrages of the segregated South. Grant Wiggins has returned with considerable ambivalence to teach in the plantation school of his childhood. He feels trapped and longs to escape with his love, another teacher named Vivian, to a place where he might breathe more freely, grow more fully, achieve something special. He had told his elderly Tante Lou, with whom he lives, "how much I hated this place and all I wanted to do was get away. I had told her I was no teacher, I hated teaching, and I was just running in place here. But she had not heard me"(pp. 14–15).

The story begins in a courtroom with Tante Lou and her lifelong friend, Miss Emma, sitting stoic and still near the front. Emma's godson, Jefferson, had been an unwitting participant in a failed liquor store stickup—his two companions and the store owner are dead—and as the sole survivor he is convicted of murder. The public defender, pleading for Jefferson's life, plays to the all-white jury with zeal:

> Gentlemen of the jury, look at this . . . boy. I almost said man, but I can't say man . . . I would call it a boy and a fool. A fool is not aware of right and wrong . . .
>
> What justice would there be to take this life? Justice gentlemen? Why I would just as soon put a hog in the electric chair as this. (p. 78)

But it's no good. Jefferson is sentenced to death. He has only a few weeks, perhaps a couple of months, to live. As devastating as the sentence is, it is that last plea from the public defender—that comparison of Jefferson to a hog—that cuts most deeply. "Called him a hog," says Miss Emma. And she turns to Grant Wiggins: "I don't want them to kill no hog" (p. 12). She wants Grant to visit Jefferson, and to teach him.

Wiggins resists: "'Yes, I'm the teacher,' I said. 'And I teach what the white folks around here tell me to teach . . . They never told me how to keep a black boy out of a liquor store'" (p. 13). More than this, Wiggins is shaken by the challenge and the context. He explains to Vivian:

> What do I say to him? Do I know how a man is supposed to die? I'm still trying to find out how a man should live. Am I supposed to tell someone how to die who has never lived? . . .
>
> Suppose . . . I reached him and made him realize that he was as much a man as any other man, then what? He's still going to die . . . so what will I have accomplished? What will I have done? Why not let the hog die without knowing anything? (p. 31)

Miss Emma and Tante Lou, along with their preacher, insist that Grant join them in their visits to Jefferson. It is an alliance filled with pain and tension—Grant has refused to go to church for years and, outspoken in his agnosticism, is looked upon by the elderly trio as, in turn, the devil himself and Jefferson's best hope. The sheriff doesn't want Grant visiting, "Because I think the only thing you can do is just aggravate him, trying to put something in his head against his will. And I'd rather see a contented hog go to that chair than an aggravated hog" (p. 49). Grant is haunted by the memory of his own former teacher, a bitter man: "You'll see that it'll take more than five and a half months to wipe away—peel—scrape away the blanket of ignorance that has been plastered and replastered over those brains in the past three hundred years. You'll see" (p. 64). The former mentor's message is that nothing a teacher in these circumstances does can matter, can make a difference. Worse than that, Jefferson himself is wracked with hopelessness; he is uncooperative, resistant: "It don't matter . . . Nothing don't matter," he says (p. 73), as he refuses to eat unless his food is put on the floor, like slops for a hog.

Grant begins by simply visiting Jefferson, being there, speaking sometimes, but mostly just sitting in silence. Witnessing. He brings Jefferson some small things: peanuts and pecans from his students, a small radio, a little notebook and a pencil. He encourages Jefferson to think of questions and write down his thoughts. And sometimes he accompanies Miss Emma, Tante Lou, and the reverend to the dayroom for visits. There he walks with Jefferson and talks to him. He encourages Jefferson to be kind to his grandmother, to eat some of the gumbo she has brought:

> I could never be a hero. I teach, but I don't like teaching. I teach because it is the only thing that an educated black man can do in the south today. I don't like it; I hate it . . . I want to live for myself and for my woman and for nobody else. . . .
>
> That is not a hero, a hero does for others . . . I am not that kind of person, but I want you to be. You could give something to her, to me, to those children in the quarter . . . The white people out there are saying that you don't have it—that you're a hog, not a man. But I know they are wrong. You have the potentials. We all have, no matter who we are . . .
>
> I want to show them the difference between what they think you are and what you can be. To them, you're nothing but another nigger—no dignity, no heart, no love for your people. You can prove them

wrong. You can do more than I can ever do. I have always done what they wanted me to do, teach reading, writing, and arithmetic. Nothing else—nothing about loving and caring. They never thought we were capable of learning those things. "Teach these niggers how to print their names and how to figure on their fingers." And I went along, but hating myself all the time for doing so . . .

White people believe that they're better than anyone else on earth—and that's a myth. The last thing they want is to see a black man stand, and think, and show that common humanity that is in us all. It would destroy their myth . . .

. . . all we are, Jefferson, all of us on this earth, [is just] a piece of drifting wood, until we—each of us, individually—decide to be something else. I am still that piece of drifting wood . . . but you can be better. Because we need you to be and want you to be . . .

He looked at me in great pain. He may not have understood, but something was touched, something deep down in him (pp. 191–193).

After Jefferson is electrocuted, a white deputy sheriff drives out to bring the news to Grant:

"He was the strongest man in that crowded room, Grant Wiggins," Paul said, staring at me and speaking louder than was necessary. "He was, he was . . . he looked at the preacher and said, 'Tell Nannan I walked.' And straight he walked, Grant Wiggins. Straight he walked" . . .

"You're one great teacher, Grant Wiggins," he said.

"I'm not great. I'm not even a teacher."

"Why do you say that?"

"You have to believe to be a teacher."

"I saw the transformation, Grant Wiggins," Paul said.

"I didn't do it."

"Who, then?"

"Maybe he did it himself."

"He never could have done that."

"I saw the transformation. I'm a witness to that." (pp. 253–254)

A Lesson Before Dying is a teacher's tale. While the circumstances are extreme, the interaction is familiar, recognizable. Every teacher appreciates the irony of teaching what we ourselves neither fully know nor understand. Each of us can remember other teachers who counseled us not to teach, and each of us recognizes the resistant student, the student who refuses to learn. And we can each uncover moments of intense self-reflection, consciousness shifts, and personal growth brought on by our attempts.

Many teachers also know what it means to teach against the grain. Against oppression, opposition, and obstinacy. Against a history of evil. Against glib, commonsense assumptions. When the sheriff compares education to agitation and the teacher to an organizer "trying to put something in his head against his will," one is reminded of Frederick Douglass's master exploding in anger when he discovers that his wife has taught the young Douglass to read: "It will unfit him to be a slave." One is reminded as well of the charge "outside agitator," hurled by the bosses at the union organizer, or by the college trustees at student radicals. When the sheriff grins at Wiggins for giving Jefferson a journal, because a hog can't write authentic thoughts or experience real human feelings, we are in a familiar space. And when Jefferson writes in the journal, "I cry 'cause you been so good to me Mr. Wiggin and nobody ain't never been that good to me an make me think I'm somebody" (p. 232). While most of us will not be lucky enough to receive such moving feedback, we recognize something fundamental about teaching.

Education of course lives an excruciating paradox precisely because of its association with and location in schools. Education is about opening doors, opening minds, opening possibilities. School is about sorting and punishing, grading and ranking and certifying. Education is unconditional—it asks nothing in return. School tends to demand obedience and conformity as a precondition to attendance. Education is surprising and unruly and disorderly, while the first and fundamental law of school is to follow orders. Education frees the mind, while schooling can bureaucratize the brain. An educator unleashes the unpredictable, while too many schoolteachers start with an unhealthy obsession with classroom management and linear lesson plans.

Working in schools, where the fundamental truths and demands and possibilities of teaching are obscure and diminished and opaque, and where the powerful ethical core of our efforts is systematically defaced and erased, requires a reengagement with the larger purposes of teaching. When the drumbeat of our daily lives is all about controlling the crowd, managing and moving the mob, conveying disembodied bits of information to inert things propped at desks before us, the need to fight for ourselves and our students becomes an imperative. Central to that fight is the understanding that there is no basis for education in a democracy except for a faith in the enduring capacity for growth in ordinary people.

In their study of contemporary American culture, *Habits of the Heart*, Robert Bellah (1985) and his colleagues make a penetrating observation about work:

> With the coming of large-scale industrial society it became more difficult to see work as a contribution to the whole and easier to view it as a segmented, self-interested activity. But though the idea of a calling has become attenuated and the largely private "job" and "career" have taken its place, something of the notion of calling lingers on, not necessarily opposed to, but in addition to job and career. In a few economically marginal, but symbolically significant instances, we can still see what a calling is. (p. 66)

Bellah's example of an economically marginal but symbolically significant worker happens to be a ballet dancer, but that description perfectly fits many teachers, those who continue to find in their work a vital link between private and public worlds, between personal fulfillment and social responsibility. They bring to their work a sense of commitment, of connectedness to other people and to shared traditions, and of collective good will. They also reject the calculation and contingency that pervade so much of work today, embodying instead a sense of work closely tied to a sense of self, a view that work is not merely what one does, but who one is. And they struggle to accomplish all of this as an act of affirmation in a social and cultural surround that devalues their contribution and rewards them sparingly.

In contrast to the dominant pattern of our society, which defines "personality, achievement, and the purpose of human life in ways that leave the individual suspended in glorious, but terrifying isolation" (Bellah et al., 1985, p. 6), for these teachers work is "morally inseparable" (p. 66) from their lives—their social commitments bend toward their private pursuits. These teachers search for ways to talk of values in an environment that constrains that talk, and to be public and political in a world that diminishes both.

These teachers seek an authentic meeting of subjects—a meeting that acknowledges the humanity, intentions, agendas, maps, dreams, desires, hopes, fears, loves, and pains of each—and in that meeting they try to model what they themselves value. They work to make explicit, at least to themselves, their own values, priorities, and stories, because they know that these things will impact teaching practice. Being aware of oneself as the instrument of one's teaching, aware, too, of the story that makes one's life sensible, allows for greater change and growth as well as greater intentionality in teaching choices.

Alice Walker writes of her co-biographical project among Black women in Mississippi:

> Slowly I am getting these stories together. Not for the public, but for the ladies who wrote them. Will seeing each other's lives make any of the past clearer to them? I don't know. I hope so. I hope contradictions will show, but also the faith and grace of a people under continuous pressure. So much of the satisfying work of life begins as an experiment; having learned this, no experiment is ever quite a failure. (p. 17)

Just so with teaching: each year, each class, each day has built within it improvisation and uncertainty, dynamism and upheaval—change. With our eyes on the larger purposes and deeper meanings of teaching, no experiment is ever quite a failure.

The complexity of the teacher's task is based on its idiosyncratic and improvisational character—as inexact as a person's mind or a human heart, as unique and inventive as a friendship or a love affair, as explosive and unpredictable as a revolution. The teacher's work is about background, environment, setting, surround, position, situation, connection. And, importantly, teaching is at its center about relationship—with this person, with our world.

Seeing the student, seeing the world—this is the beginning: to assume a deep capacity in students, an intelligence (often obscure, sometimes buried) as well as a wide range of hopes, dreams, and aspirations; to acknowledge, as well, obstacles to understand and overcome, deficiencies to repair, injustices to correct. With this as a base, the teacher creates an environment for learning that has multiple entry points for learning and multiple pathways to success. That environment must be abundant with opportunities to practice ethical action; to display, foster, embody, expect, demand, nurture, allow, model, and enact inquiry toward a moral universe. A classroom organized in this way follows a particular rhythm: questions focus on issues or problems (What do we need or want to know? Why is it important? How will we find out?), and on action (Given what we know now, what are we going to do?).

In every classroom, in every situation and project, I try to bring to bear my own evolving core commitments, to live my larger purposes and deepest goals. Thinking in terms of core commitments isn't a bad way to begin—it can help each of us to manage the complex challenges we face, and to stay awake to unforeseen possibilities. For me, making my commitments explicit can provide guideposts for my teaching and my advocacy:

- *The visibility of persons.* Each person is induplicable, the one and only who will ever walk the earth, and each must be approached with reverence and awe. Every human life is valuable beyond measure, each a whole universe. I want to resist the reductive enterprise of labeling, the fragmentation of living, breathing, trembling human beings into a set of pathologies to remediate. In my work I want to think in terms of solidarity, not service, of identification *with* rather than identification *of.* I believe that at bottom the people with the problems are also the people with the solutions.
- *Wide awake and aware.* The world is not only complex and difficult, but it is also a place in desperate need of repair. I want to make a concrete analysis of real conditions so that I can be fully engaged in life as it's lived. I believe that the opposite of moral isn't always immoral—more commonly, the opposite of moral is indifferent.
- *Rethinking.* I want to resist the temptation to dissolve into automatic thinking, received wisdom, and dogma. I went to be agnostic, skeptical of me and hopeful of us, and I want to cultivate my imagination so that I can pursue alternatives. All of this encourages me to continually push beyond the comfort zone of my home and my experience. I believe that exile provides both a wider and truer angle of regard as well as an opportunity for more solid human connections.
- *Link consciousness to conduct.* We need to know what's happening in the world in order to know what to oppose and what to support, who to embrace and how. But it's not enough to know, we must also act. And when we act we must also doubt. I believe this is an essential rhythm: learn, act, doubt, in an endless circle.

These essays are loosely collected around examining the contemporary conditions of schooling, the issues teachers face every day
in today's schools, the problem of professionalism and the challenges
to teacher educators. In the last section I return to what I consider
the heart of the matter: teachers teaching. Together these essays
point to teaching as an intellectual and ethical enterprise, a relational
enterprise geared to the formation of identity and the fulfillment of
our deepest humanity. Teaching as an ethical enterprise goes beyond
presenting what already is; it is teaching toward what ought to be.
It is more than moral structures and guidelines; it includes an exposure to and understanding of material realities—advantages and
disadvantages, privileges and oppressions—as well. Teaching of this
kind might stir people to come together as vivid, thoughtful, and,
yes, even outraged. Students, then, might find themselves dissatisfied with what had only yesterday seemed the natural order of
things. At this point, when consciousness links to conduct and upheaval is in the air, teaching becomes a call to freedom.

The fundamental message of the teacher, after all, is this: you
can change your life. Whoever you are, wherever you've been,
whatever you've done, the teacher invites you to a second chance,
another round, perhaps a different conclusion. The teacher posits
possibility, openness, and alternative; the teacher points to what
could be, but is not yet. The teacher beckons you to change your
path, and so the teacher's basic rule is to reach.

To teach consciously for ethical action adds an essential element
to that fundamental message, making it more layered, more dense,
more excruciatingly difficult to enact, and at the same time sturdier,
more engaging, more powerful and joyful much of the time. Teaching for ethical action demands a dialectical stance: one eye firmly
fixed on the students—Who are they? What are their hopes, dreams,
and aspirations, their passions and commitments? What skills, abilities, and capacities does each one bring to the classroom?—and the
other eye looking unblinkingly at the concentric circles of context—
historical flow, cultural surrounding, economic reality. Teaching as
an ethical enterprise is teaching that arouses students, engages
them in a quest to identify obstacles to their full humanity and the
life chances of others, to their freedom, and then to drive, to move
against those obstacles. And so the fundamental message of the
teacher for ethical action is this: You must change the world. Teach-

ing is the extraordinary work of ordinary people, worthy of our attention, our support, our dedication.

Pablo Neruda's "The Poet's Obligation," written for his fellow poets, sketches the potential power of a life in teaching:

> To whoever is not listening to the sea
> this Friday morning, to whoever is cooped up
> in house or office, factory . . .
> or street or mine or dry prison cell,
> to him I come, and without speaking or looking
> I arrive and open the door of his prison,
> and a vibration starts up, vague and insistent,
> a long rumble of thunder adds itself
> to the weight of the planet and the foam,
> the groaning rivers of the ocean rise,
> the star vibrates quickly in its corona
> and the sea beats, dies, and goes on beating.
>
> So, drawn on by my destiny,
> I ceaselessly must listen to and keep
> the sea's lamenting in my consciousness,
> I must feel the crash of the hard water
> and gather it up in a perpetual cup
> so that, wherever those in prison may be,
> wherever they suffer the sentence of the autumn,
> I may be present with an errant wave.
> I move in and out of windows,
> and hearing me, eyes may lift themselves,
> asking "How can I reach the sea?"
> And I will pass to them, saying nothing,
> the starry echoes of the wave,
> a breaking up of foam and quicksand,
> a resulting of salt withdrawing itself,
> the gray cry of sea birds on the coast.
>
> So, through me, freedom and the sea
> will call in answer to the shrouded heart.

PART I

CONTEMPORARY CONDITIONS OF SCHOOLING AND TEACHING

The schools we have are neither acts of God nor the consequence of the normal workings of the natural world. They are neither inspired nor accidental. Rather, our schools are entirely human constructions, the result of the actions and inactions of people, the deeds and misdeeds, wisdom and ignorance of our fellow citizens. Even as they appear before us as somehow immutable, as solid and inevitable, as a final destination, we would do well to remind ourselves that today's schools were built by people like ourselves— complex and contradictory, both fated and free—that schools as we know them are rather recent inventions, and that anything done by people can be undone and redone by other people. We are not merely victims of our circumstances and objects of our time; we can also become actors and subjects in the forward-changing, ongoing human drama.

This section invites you to consider the contemporary conditions of schooling, from the savage inequalities that condemn so many children to classrooms of hopelessness and despair, to the luminous hopeful schools built on assumptions of human capacity, a determination to fight back against injustice. The point here is to face reality, but simultaneously refuse to accede to it too easily.

CHAPTER 2

Teaching for Justice and Care

"What is it," I asked several urban school administrators, "about the presence of large numbers of poor, African American or immigrant city kids in your schools that makes those places wonderful?"

Silence. Several looks of disbelief. Some nervous laughter. And then this: "Our jobs are hard enough without you ridiculing us."

The question was not meant to ridicule, but rather to disconnect an unexamined and glib fiction about city kids. It's true that the last word—*wonderful*—sounds a decidedly discordant note. Until then the question hums along quite comfortably, a familiar melody. But when the anticipated last bar—something like *terrible,* or *difficult,* or, at best, *challenging*—is not delivered, the whole thing sounds out of tune.

An assumption that sits heavy and dogmatic on most city schools is that there is nothing about the presence of African-American youngsters—especially, in today's environment, African-American boys—that is deemed valuable, hopeful, or important. Their attendance in school is an encumbrance. They are an obstruction, a handicap, and a burden. If these youngsters are known at all, they are known by their deficits and their presumed inadequacies. School becomes, then, entirely a matter of remediation and repair. Good intentions notwithstanding, feelings of hopelessness and despair begin to define these places for students and teachers alike. There is, then, a diminishing space where justice and care might come alive.

I was asked once to look at hundreds of applications filled out by teachers who had been nominated for an outstanding teacher award in Chicago. One question asked, "What is the biggest obstacle in your teaching?" Nearly half the respondents answered in one way or another that the students were the biggest obstacle. Not everyone just blurted it out. Many said things like, "I used to be a better teacher, but kids today have so many problems." Some wrote, "If these kids could only speak English . . ." But it all added up to a powerful message that schools and classrooms would function much, much better if the students would simply not show up. Picture the perfect city school: classrooms are always quiet, the cafeteria always calm, the hallways always orderly. No fights, no hassles, no graffiti. Bells ring, xerox machines hum, paychecks are delivered. The place is efficient, clean, peaceful. No kids? No problem. Within this environment, to even raise the question of the value of city kids is to sound slightly mad.

Most city teachers struggle mightily to do a good job in spite of inadequate resources and difficult circumstances—indeed, the structure of most city schools (the strict schedule, the division of knowledge, the press of time, the pretense of rational efficiency, and the huge number of students—all leading to a factory-like operation characterized by hierarchy, control, and anonymity) works to turn teachers into clerks, and students into objects to fear and coerce. Clerks (and clerk-teachers) are not expected to think too deeply or care too much. Thoughtlessness and carelessness undermine education—they also damage democracy, justice, and an ethic of caring. Engagement, thoughtfulness, connectedness, valuing youngsters as three-dimensional beings with their own hopes, dreams, and capacities to build upon—these are the basics in teaching toward democracy and justice and care.

When I think of teaching for justice and care, I think beyond the classroom to teachers like Jane Addams. Addams was one of our greatest dissenters: a socialist, early feminist, pacifist, and activist. She has been sanitized and defanged with the rosy glow of history, but it is important to remember that she was a fighter and a builder, that she did not follow a path already laid out. When she established Hull House in Chicago over a century ago, she argued that building communities of care and compassion required more than "doing good," more than volunteerism, more than the controlling stance of the benefactor. It required human solidarity, a oneness with others in distress. She had this in mind when she opened her settlement house, lived there with families of crisis and need, and saw the world through their eyes.

There are countless teachers today sweating out Jane Addams's hopes, naming situations and circumstances as unacceptable, acting on their own consciousness and concern to repair deficiencies, to

right wrongs. A Chicago teacher-photographer named Leise Ricketts, for example, initiated a project she calls Drive-By Peace. She
distributes cameras to young people in housing projects and teaches
them after school and on weekends the art of her craft, the tools of
her trade. Her first assignment is for the kids to photograph a safe
place. Recently one youngster took a picture of his room, another
her mother's lap, a third the cover of a favorite book. Ricketts is pos-
iting peace and safety as possible, something to identify, expand, and
strive for.

Jamie Kalven, a teacher, writer, and activist, created a program
called Turn-A-Lot-Around, a Chicago citizen action project in which
vacant lots are turned into gardens and playgrounds, one lot at a
time, through the collective physical labor of neighbors. Kalven is
expanding the notion of environmental racism even as he names
space and labor as two wasted resources in the city.

And Hal Adams, a colleague and friend, has built a stunning
adult literacy project in which mothers in poor city neighborhoods
are writing autobiographical sketches and portraits, in the process
making problems that had been constructed exclusively as personal
and private become public, shared, and social. This literacy project
has developed other dimensions—*Real Conditions* is an irregular
publication of their writings, used as a reader in some classrooms,
distributed throughout the community. The participants, having
found common cause, have also discovered social and political dimensions to their work. They have struggled together to close a
crack house, for example, and to rid their community of guns. They
have hosted readings and authors' nights in public libraries. Literacy has become for them a vehicle for deeper participation as citizens, and learning to read has been linked to claiming and even
changing the world.

These wildly diverse projects, each the work of a city teacher,
have certain common edges. Each is built on a sense of dialogue and
not monologue; teachers expect to be changed, not merely to bring
change. Each assumes an intelligence in people; each sees and
builds upon possibility and not merely deficit. Each is premised on
solidarity and not service, on a sense of community as shared and
constructed and proven, not merely proclaimed.

When we contemplate democracy and justice in urban schools,
we might consider the ways in which the system itself is a model of

injustice, an obstacle to democracy. Although it is possible to think in an environment of thoughtlessness and to care in a time of care-lessness—to create a classroom of justice and care within a world of oppression and cruelty—it's also true that thought and care are di-minished in subtle and overt ways when larger social forces and structures act to undermine them. For example, the inequitable dis-tribution of educational resources leaves most city schools starved and desperate (Chicago's DuSable High School, in the shadow of Robert Taylor Homes, spends $6,000 per year per child; the North Shore's New Trier High School spends $12,000); the existence of a range of tangled and self-interested bureaucracies sitting atop city schools, each capable of working its own narrow will against any notion of the common good, renders many schools lifeless places, hopeless and gutless; the presence of a culture of contempt for city kids, distant from communities and families, deadens students and weakens teachers.

Not surprisingly, this unnatural, selective school crisis is a crisis of the poor, of the cities, of Latino and African-American commu-nities. All the structures of privilege and oppression apparent in the larger society are mirrored and mimicked in our schools: Chicago public school students, for example, are overwhelmingly children of color—65% are African American, 25% are Latino. They are children of the poor—68% qualify for federal lunch programs. More than half of the poorest children in Illinois (and over two-thirds of the state's bilingual children) attend Chicago schools. And yet Chicago schools must struggle to educate children with consid-erably less human and material resources than neighboring districts.

The purpose of education in a democracy is to break down bar-riers, to overcome obstacles, to, as Deborah Meier wrote in her jour-nal, "believe the startling proposition that we are all created equal" (Meier, 1995, p. 2), and to embody that belief. Education is em-powering and enabling; it points to strength, to critical capacity, to thoughtfulness and expanding capabilities. It aims at something deeper and richer than simply imbibing and accepting the codes and conventions of the time, acceding to whatever common sense soci-ety posits. The larger goal of education is to assist people in seeing the world through their own eyes, interpreting and analyzing through their own experiences and reflective thinking, feeling themselves capable of representing, manifesting, or even, if they choose, changing what they find before them. Education at its best, then, is linked to freedom, to the ability to see but also to alter, to understand but also to reinvent, to know and also to transform the world. Can we imagine this at the core of city schools?

If city school systems are to be retooled, streamlined, and made workable, if they are to become palaces of learning for all children (Why not? Why does *palaces* sound so provocatively extravagant?), then we must fight for a comprehensive program of change. To begin, educational resources must be distributed fairly, and justice, the notion that all children deserve a decent life, that the greatest need deserves the greatest support, must become our guide.

Further, school people need to find common cause with students and parents. We must remake schools by drawing on strengths and capacities in communities, rather than by focusing obsessively on deficiencies and difficulties. We must name our problems as shared and social, and our solutions as collective and manageable. We must note that the people with the problems are also the people essential to creating the solutions, and we must act accordingly.

Most of all we must, each and all of us, get angry at the injustices and the obstacles, and become proactive in opening new possibilities. Anyone who is waiting for someone else to get it right (the union, the school board, the legislature, the mayor) before taking action will likely wait forever. The challenge is to act, to build whatever alliances we can, to change this corner of this school right now.

Powerful learning projects begin with learners, and knowing city kids as learners, discovering them as multidimensional beings, as fellow creatures, is an important place for teachers to begin. What experiences, knowledge, and skills do children bring with them to school? What kinds of thought and intelligence are there to challenge and nurture? A sustained engagement with these questions is a basic starting point for city teachers. And it is followed closely by the demand to create an environment for learning that is wide enough and deep enough to nourish and engage the huge range of students who actually walk through the classroom door (as opposed to the fantasy student, the stereotype student, ingrained in our consciousness from too many years of *Leave It to Beaver* or *Beverly Hills, 90210*). This means there must be multiple entry points to learning, a variety of ways to begin, an assortment of pathways to success. And it points toward another complex teaching task: building bridges of understanding between the experiences and knowledge young-sters bring with them into the classroom toward deeper and wider ways of knowing. An excruciatingly difficult task, but the whole dynamic enterprise begins with knowing the student.

Teachers need to be intensely aware of what they value, what they honor, what they stand for. Even with this awareness, the machinery of schooling works on teachers like water on rock: it wears us down, shapes us, and smoothes us. Soon, if we're not careful, our lives begin to make a mockery of our values. Resisting this fate involves conscious struggle, an attempt to find allies among the students, the parents, the teachers, and the citizenry. It requires collective action. It requires wedding consciousness to conduct, and it involves taking responsibility for ourselves, for our work, for the world we see and can understand, and a world that could be but is not yet. The essential challenge to city teachers is to make education take root and bloom full flower on the hard surfaces of urban schools. That is our task, and nothing less will do.

CHAPTER 3

Classroom Spaces, Teacher Choices

Among Schoolchildren, Tracy Kidder's popular account of one year in the life of Chris Zajac's classroom—well written, highly praised, depressingly familiar—is all style, no substance. We are introduced, for example, to a typical rash of colds and flu as "small epidemics [that] passed though the class, and children with puffy eyes and reddened noses, walking Petri dishes, were driven home by outreach workers, leaving temporary holes in the room" (Kidder, 1989, p. 117). We meet a long line of engaging students such as Judith, Mrs. Zajac's "shiniest hope," a "Puerto Rican child who could certainly succeed on the mainland, and on mainland terms." The book is completely white bread (p. 318).

Kidder takes his readers on the shortest of journeys: an anesthetizing trip back to school. It's a well-known world, and everything in it is immediately recognizable. Here's the principal: "Al would lean slightly backward, arms folded on his chest, and bark at the first signs of mischief. 'Hey you! Yeah, you! Excuse me! Stay in line with your mouth shut!'" (1989, p. 45).

And teacher meetings: "Al dragged out meetings. Sometimes he gave his teachers printed handouts and then read the contents to them" (p. 45).

Here is the teacher: "'Out!' she said. The imperious teacher finger pointed toward the door. 'I'm going to leave him out there till he rots,' she said to herself" (p. 204).

And the student teacher: "At the end of a day in October, Pam said to Chris, 'I don't know how you do it.' Pam looked sad. 'You just come in and they're quiet'" (p. 116).

Here are the students: "There were twenty children. About half were Puerto Rican. Almost two-thirds of the twenty needed the forms to obtain free lunches. There was a lot of long and curly hair. Some boys wore little rattails . . . Their faces ranged from dark brown to gold, to pink, to pasty white, the color that Chris associated with sunless tenements and too much TV . . . There was a lot of prettiness in the room, and all of the children looked cute to Chris" (p. 6).

And, of course, the environment for learning: "At eight, a high-pitched beep from the intercom announced math which lasted an hour" (p. 28); "On the bulletin boards in the hallways, Halloween displays lingered almost until Thanksgiving. Most of the displays were store bought or inspired by books of ideas for bulletin boards, on sale at all stores that cater to teachers" (p. 128).

Even the book's jacket is seductive, lulling the reader to settle into one of the little wooden desks in a classroom with the green chalkboard and its multiplication problem, the old school clock, the public-address speaker, the American flag and the teacher's desk and chair at the front. *Among Schoolchildren* is the taken-for-granted cliché in stupefying detail—an amplification of its stereotyped jacket illustration. There is absolutely no demonstration of a critical eye at work, evidence neither of insight nor serious inquiry. Problems appear in Kidder's picture, of course, but they are outside his story and beyond his scope. In Kidder's world everything just *is*— immutable facts, universal conditions, undeniable events. He challenges nothing.

Teaching is an intensely interactive enterprise with complex intellectual challenges and ongoing ethical choices. Kidder acknowledges the complexity of teaching without ever explicitly locating it. "Decades of research and reform have not altered the fundamental facts of teaching," (p. 53) he reports. These fundamental facts are women alone in classrooms, the press of time, the impossibly wide range of kids, the elusive rewards, homework, classroom management, unreasonable demands, and inadequate resources.

Kidder's hero struggles on—but not *against* these "fundamental facts of teaching" (p. 53). She accedes totally. When her student teacher observes that Clarence is being hurt by "the structure of the school" and that he "just wants to move around," Chris explains that "this is what there is." Kidder says, "She has no choice" (p. 102). This becomes Kidder's essential theme, his mantra, the backdrop for interpreting Chris Zajac's world: no choice.

The no-choice theme makes for bestseller material. It's comfortable. In a culture that promotes obedience and conformity, in a society where freedom means choosing which television channel to watch, which brand name to buy, or which expressway to drive along, it's an easy fit. Don't worry, be happy. Authentic choices are always troublesome and problematic. No choice, no problem.

This theme constantly collides with an alternative sense of teaching, teaching as urgent questioning and continuous choice-making, teaching as a creative act. The book trembles with unasked questions: When Chris moves Felipe's desk because he is "chattering too much," (p. 17) what is he chattering about? When she keeps a group of children in from recess for failing to do their homework, what had the homework been? And when she sets the goal of getting the troubled Clarence not only to "do his work" (really her work) but to "like school and schoolwork someday," (p. 19) what is there about it to like? Again and again and again, what else could she do?

When Zajac sighs, "All I want to do is teach. I want a quiet afternoon so I can teach," (p. 223) she is longing to stand in front of the class, to deliver the goods from her lesson plans, to have all hands busy, all mouths closed, and all eyes on her. To act but not to interact. The teacher as lecturer. The teacher as clerk. Her desire is both common and understandable, perhaps, but also mistaken.

Real teaching is messy. It involves an authentic meeting, an engagement between teacher and learners. Teachers must know their students, reach out to them with care and understanding in order to create a bridge from the known to the not-yet-known. Teaching that is more than incidental, more than accidental, demands sustained empathetic regard. Teaching is initially the art of invitation, and it is virtually impossible to invite people to learn if they are strange or inscrutable to you. Good teachers find ways to know and understand learners. They observe and record students at work and at play. They create dialogue. They inquire. They map social and cultural contexts. Odd or unfamiliar contexts place a straightforward demand upon the teacher: Become a student of your own students as a prerequisite to teaching them. Good teaching is a continuous inquiry into students and learning, an endless engagement with a basic question: Given what I now know, how will I teach this student?

When I asked some student teachers to study a child in their classrooms, to diagram the class and the school, and to map the neighborhoods, the wider context of learning, to find out where people worked, shopped, played, ate, and so on, one student said, "I would only map that neighborhood from the passenger seat of my father's squad car." My response was that there was no way she could successfully engage children she feared or hated.

Some teachers begin with a belief that teaching is telling, talking, cajoling, or coercing: teachers know, students don't know, teachers teach, students learn. Some teachers also assume that kids should be automatically eager, attentive, and interested in everything dictated by the teacher or the state legislature or the curriculum guide. These teachers spend their time looking at themselves, at their performance, and not at the kids. They feel betrayed by the complexity of actual teaching and the trembling reality of living kids. They then sometimes blame parents and whole communities. They come to think that the biggest obstacle to their teaching is the children themselves. Some teachers say, "I used to be a great teacher, but I can't teach *these* kids," or "I would be a wonderful teacher if I had better kids."

Kidder's Zajac is not that transparent. She goes on trying with her students and their families, but with her cultural blinders firmly fixed: "Clarence's life outside school seemed too distant even to imagine" (Kidder, 1989, p. 105). "The boy's so bright! If only I could change the circumstances of his life" (p. 290); "Robert's mother . . . said, 'This school hasn't done nothing' for him . . . ' Chris kept wishing she had said, 'At least we've tried, lady!'" (p. 213); Clarence's mother "wore a colorful cloth bandanna wound around her temples. She was tall. Her voice was deep. She looked exotic and powerful, and maybe even dangerous if crossed" (p. 177); "What's in the cats is in the kittens, as my mother likes to say" (p. 212). For all the spunk and effort and good humor, an abiding contempt defeats any higher teaching purposes. Instead of regarding children's cultures, communities, and families as assets in her teaching, Zajac assumes that all that they are must be rejected as a step toward becoming cultured, civilized. Instead of tapping into experience and attitude and background, Zajac worries about "losing them back to their environment" (p. 330).

The art of teaching begins with understanding learners and then goes on to create an environment that is complex enough and rich enough to nurture and challenge a wide range of interests, experiences, purposes, and aspirations. Teaching is about enabling others in some way, making people more powerful. Teachers must stay alive to the fundamental curriculum question: What knowledge and experiences are of most value? And teachers must then ask themselves the basic teaching question: What kind of environment, what routines and rhythms and resources, will allow students access to those valuable experiences and that worthwhile knowledge? None of this is ever static, straightforward, or finished. These questions frame the always inexact, forever improvisational dance of teaching.

A decent environment for learning is interactive, flexible, growing, and co-constructed. It is aesthetically pleasing and alive. When the only potted plant in Chris Zajac's classroom dies, she mockingly hums a funeral dirge as she dumps it in the garbage and says, "I don't have time to water plants." She is limiting her students and herself with her painfully constrained view of curriculum and environment. Students can, if allowed and encouraged, help build a learning environment that includes familiar as well as unfamiliar things. If students don't know what's available, the environment is not useful. If they must wait endlessly to satisfy their interests or curiosities, it is self-defeating. If they are expected to receive instead of construct knowledge, it is hopelessly misguided.

Tracy Kidder describes curriculum guides, subjects divided into one-hour or half-hour blocks, tracked reading groups, the ritualistic class trip, art lessons such as copying Easter bunnies onto paper, social studies lesson where "Chris elaborates on how slavery hurts everyone, including auctioneers." The science fair has no recognizable link to science, and Chris looks, typically, in the wrong direction: "Chris felt a secret relief. She had awakened one night not long ago imaging children from other classes standing behind wonderful homemade rocket ships and expounding on physics, while her students explained to fairgoers, 'This is a potato' and 'These are rocks.' Chris told herself now, 'At least I don't feel too embarrassed. Mine aren't any worse than anyone else's'" (1989, p. 277).

There is a maddening disregard for children's feelings, insights, and questions here. The children are routinely ignored, made to feel inadequate, stupid, weak, or bad in school, and yet the focus never leaves the teacher. Robert is humiliated in the science fair, and his vulnerability endears him to Chris: he "seemed to recover fast," while "Chris's recovery took longer" (p. 284). Why does Kidder think so? Because Robert walks around the gym "making shaky movements with his hands"? (p. 289). When Jimmy tells Mrs. Zajac that being called on makes him feel stupid, she dismisses his insight and critique by insisting that he is not stupid. Why can't she listen to him explain that her teaching has had this effect on him?

The dramatic heart of the book involves the decision to send Clarence out of Mrs. Zajac's class to Alpha, a special school with an "evil reputation" (p. 167). Clarence has been a problem from the start, and the buildup begins early: "It was usually better at first to let her own opinions form. But she couldn't help noticing the thickness of some cumes [cumulative records]. . . . Clarence's cume was about as thick as the Boston phone book" (p. 8).

Clarence refuses to do schoolwork and is impervious to the usual threats and punishments. "Chris told him gently that if he didn't he couldn't go to gym. That didn't make Clarence comply" (p. 98). Instead, he fights and rips up some materials. The struggle is long and intense, but it ends in banishment: "Sending Clarence to Alpha seemed like a decision to accomplish something that was probably right by doing something that was probably wrong" (p. 167). This twisted thinking follows the dominant logic of schools as sorting machines, as factories.

Chris resists the decision but is beaten down. Al, the principal, explains that he "can't let a teacher go up there and say, 'Oh, no, I can't send him there.' It's not for her to make that decision" (pp. 167–168). Whose decision is it? As in any bureaucracy, the decision is made by committee—it's the prototypical rule by no one. Clarence, his family, and Chris may be consulted, but they can never decide. The decision must have at least the pretense of objectivity: "Too much feeling for a boy like Clarence would only get in the way of what she wanted to do for him" (p. 159). Hmmmm . . .

Following the decision to send Clarence away, Chris tries to put the best face on it. On Clarence's last day in class she suggests that the students write in their journals how they feel about his leaving. When Felipe says, "He said the reason he's leaving is because you told him to," Chris responds disingenuously, "Well, there were a lot of people involved. We all thought it was the best thing for him" (p. 187). No one's buying it, certainly not Clarence. In the very saddest moment in this very sad book, Chris urges Clarence to give Alpha a chance. "Nope," he says. Chris perseveres: "'The teacher seemed nice, didn't she? Why don't you want to go? What's so bad about the school? Tell me what you don't like about it. I think you'll like it. I really do.' He just kept shaking his head" (p. 189). It's not enough to hurt Clarence, he must somehow thank the school for it. He refuses.

The Clarence experience shakes Zajac up. She doubts herself and the school. Doubt is in fact part of good teaching. Good teachers maintain a tension between critical doubt and forgiveness: without forgiveness the complexity of teaching is overwhelming, but without that doubt teachers become apologists for the status quo. Here Zajac raises tentative questions. "She brooded on the general question: why did the poorest children seem to learn the least in school?" (p. 200). Al tries to cheer everyone up at the teachers' meeting: "We can't bring them all up to grade level no matter what we do . . . But can we improve instruction here? You bet we can" (p. 199). Kidder points out that Zajac's problems are not philosophical or general, and that she must take stock of the particular problems she faces. In taking stock, she discovers that "most had made normal progress" and "normal measures would carry them along" (p. 201). On the verge of real questioning, Kidder and Zajac sweep everything under the carpet. Their reassurance is glib and self-congratulatory.

Janet Malcolm's controversial and gripping account of Joe McGinnis's journalistic adventure in the Jeffrey MacDonald murder case, *The Journalist and the Murderer* (1990), has an in-your-face opening: "Every journalist who is not too stupid or too full of himself to notice what is going on knows that what he does is morally indefensible. He is a kind of confidence man, preying on people's vanity, ignorance, or loneliness, gaining their trust and betraying them without remorse" (p. 3). Tracy Kidder knows all about this. His portrait is grotesque and ultimately dishonest. His Chris Zajac, earnest, hard-working, often hopeful, usually wrong in her teaching choices, is a fiction. Kidder has found something familiar and created someone believable. But *Among Schoolchildren* is pop ethnography and rip-off research. He takes no responsibility for raising the right questions or participating in better outcomes. His close observation and detailed recording are stereotyped. Mostly the book lacks an ethical core.

Compared to Sylvia Ashton-Warner's *Teacher,* Herbert Kohl's *36 Children* or *Growing Minds,* John Holt's *Learning All the Time,* Mike Rose's *Lives on the Boundary,* or Phillip Lopate's *Being with Children*—each a book by a teacher, a person who must take the risks and live with the consequences—Kidder's book conveys no sense of really being there. Kidder wants to do good, but he is not likely to roll up his sleeves and engage in the requisite hard work. He is a tourist and a dilettante, a voyeur.

In mythologizing a classroom and a teacher, Tracy Kidder has obfuscated a system of commonsense control and institutionalized oppression, a system that has trapped Clarence, Robert, Jimmy, Judith, and Chris Zajac herself in a predictable spiral of failure. Kidder's story is a misty-eyed account of a situation that fails all children some of the time and some children all of the time. Teachers should vow to resist that failure. We need to reject the frightful scripts that have already been written; we must find ways to become authors of our own teaching stories, creators of our own teacher paths.

CHAPTER 4

Savage Inequalities:
Children in America's Schools

A 14-year-old girl from East St. Louis, Illinois, says, "We have a school . . . named for Dr. King. The school is full of sewer water and the doors are locked with chains. Every student in that school is black. It's like a terrible joke on history" (Kozol, 1991, p, 35).

A Hispanic student from the South Bronx says, "People on the outside may think we don't know what it is like for other students, but we visit other schools and we have eyes and we have brains. You cannot hide the differences. You see it and compare" (p. 104).

These are two of the many voices that frame Jonathan Kozol's moving, shocking, and important *Savage Inequalities* (1991), an account of his 2-year investigation into the neighborhoods and schools of the privileged and the disadvantaged. The book combines interviews with extensive descriptions of school facilities and classroom practices, as well as detailed analyses of school policies and finances.

Kozol's powerful portrait of American education is not a pretty picture. He argues that the system is firmly and insistently separate and unequal, a dual society in which "social policy has been turned back almost 100 years" (p. 4). Piece by piece, bit by bit, he builds the case until it becomes entirely credible and compelling: as a result of indifference and political determination, greed, public policy, and racism, we have created in the United States one set of public schools that gives some of its students access to a world of choice, power, and possibility, and a separate system of schools that dramatically narrows a child's options. Schools that work are largely for White, affluent, upper- or middle-class children, while schools that fail are reserved for children of color and poverty.

Certainly, the system has its defenders. Former Illinois governor James Thompson, in a commentary on Chicago public schools, said

"We can't keep throwing money into a black hole" (Jelloun, 1999, p. 163). Presumably, Chicago's magnet schools, which get more funding dollars than most neighborhood schools, are not black holes, and so resources spent there are not squandered. Presumably, New Trier High School, with its 26-acre campus encompassing seven gymnasiums, an Olympic-size swimming pool, and a faculty advisor for every 25 youngsters, is not a black hole. Instead, Chicago's DuSable High School, which is crowded into a city block and has one lone counselor for every 420 students, is where we don't want "to throw money" (political vernacular otherwise expressed as "to appropriate funds" or "to designate resources").

Although Kozol understands that a range of other factors contribute to our education crisis—including but not limited to stifling bureaucracies, the conservative and deadening culture of most schools, and inadequate teacher education—he has chosen to focus his piercing gaze on the grossly inequitable distribution of educational resources, and to document the devastating impact that this has on children.

How do schools reflect the difference between big-spending and bare-bones districts? One school has state-of-the-art science equipment, while another lacks even a single lab; one offers Latin and six foreign languages, while another doesn't have a set of books to go around; one has a student-run TV station, while another has no toilet paper and no doors to the lavatories.

And what are the consequences of these savage inequalities? Our schools successfully sort children into winners and losers. More devastating, says Kozol, our schools convince students in some absolute, moral sense, they deserve to fail.

The heartbreaking fact is that children deserve neither their privileges nor their oppression. Public education holds out the promise that one's life is neither fully prescribed nor entirely scripted, that there is something worthwhile to strive and to live for. *Savage Inequalities* explodes that myth. It challenges us to take action toward the achievable goal of a decent school system for all, an essential condition for a moral universe, the necessary frame of a democratic and a just society.

CHAPTER 5

Schools That Work

When I was elected national education secretary of Students for a Democratic Society (SDS) in the 1960s, I got a congratulatory phone call from my father. He had seen me on the news, he told me, and while he did not like what either I or my comrades had said, he thought that I, next to them, was at least civil and articulate. Form above content, I thought. And then he said something that offered a glimpse into a deeper, more substantive disagreement: "Why do you call yourselves students *for* a democratic society," he asked, "when this already *is* a democratic society?" I felt the gulf widening.

SDS was a creature of its time—we fought for civil rights and marched for peace, organized among the poor and built a strong radical presence on campuses across the country. We practiced an irregular politics of militancy and theater, and while we enacted a range of tactics and strategies—some of us tried to build a counter-society of free schools, free expressions, free food, and full participation within the boundaries of what we thought of as a dying culture, others of us blasted away at power—we were guided by a strong ethos that none of us (in this country and, indeed, in the world) could be free until all were free, and that consciousness must be linked with conduct. In other words, we were aiming toward a dynamic notion of participatory democracy, both in the movement we were gropingly inventing and in the larger society we felt compelled to change. The test of our ideas about reform or revolution was practice, the experiential field we continually mined to guide our next steps.

George Wood, founder of the Institute for Democracy and Education in Athens, Ohio, carries on the fight for a democratic society today. Through an annual conference he sponsors of activists and democratic educators, co-editing the journal *Democracy and Education*, and his important new book, *Schools That Work: America's*

Most Innovative Public Education Programs (1992), Wood nurtures the impulses he finds in schools toward a more robust civic culture, connects and enlarges the local efforts of many, and makes the case for democratic schools as a cornerstone of a revitalized democratic society. For Wood, theory is a guide, not a prison, and his thinking is clear and accessible:

> What does democratic life require of us? What of those things can we affect in the schools? Fundamentally, democracy requires citizens who participate broadly in informed public decision-making with an eye toward the common good. Citizens must thus be literate, able not only to master the rudiments of reading, writing, and computing, but able to use these tools as ways of understanding the world and making their voices heard in it. We must also know how to find and evaluate information, how to sift through the items that bombard us daily, to sort the useful from the superfluous, the clearly propagandistic from the approximate truths . . . Citizens should see themselves as members of a community that makes their individuality possible, and they should value and nurture that community. Democracy also requires that we each have courage, that we believe our actions are important and valued, and that we have not only a right, but an obligation to participate publicly. (1992, p. xviii)

Wood describes the kind of schools that would assist in the creation of public citizens: places where the dreams, aspirations, knowledge, and skills of youth are sensible starting points for learning; places where students and teachers alike find socially meaningful and intellectually challenging work to do; places where people are treated as valuable and where they find ways to become people of values; places where children can read critically, speak openly, and think freely; places where everyone can participate in the life of the community and find ways to make a difference. In other words, schools where democracy is lived and not merely talked about, practiced rather than ritualized.

George Wood finds living models of these democratic spaces in public schools across America, and he sketches powerful, nuanced portraits of democratic education in practice. Places like La Escuela Fratney in Milwaukee, a two-way bilingual, multicultural elementary school where the curriculum is organized around themes like "Our Roots in the School and the Community" and "We Are a Multicultural Nation"; places like Central Park East Secondary School in Spanish Harlem, where teachers build their teaching around questions designed to develop critical dispositions of mind—How do we know what we know? What's the evidence? What's the viewpoint? How else may it be considered? What difference does it make?

In these schools we see youngsters acquiring a range of skills and engaging in deeply serious intellectual work, all in the context of larger purposes and deeper goals. Writing is undertaken, for example, in light of the need to tell a story, to make known a point of view, or to organize a petition drive, rather than as an arbitrary, punitive, or disconnected bit of schoolwork, something to get over and done with as another exercise in pointlessness.

Of course, if this kind of dynamic, purposeful education can exist in some public schools, why not in all? If these schools have found ways to engage the interests and respond to the needs of a wide range of youngsters with troubling backgrounds and difficult circumstances, why can't the rest?

George Wood describes possibilities, and he argues that the fight for decent schools is part of a larger struggle to create a more humane and just social order. The schools are an important venue for struggle because they are among the last public spaces where large numbers of people gather in mutual need and common pursuit. Schools reflect the social order, including every contradiction and germ of something hopeful growing within people, and that, too, makes them a sensible site for a movement for democracy. Public schools in particular are places where the language of freedom catches abruptly on the policy of obedience, where the dissonance between faith and fact grates most painfully.

George Wood is an unapologetically political person, but for him politics is neither dissembling opportunism nor narrow self-interest. He aims in part to rescue politics from its current meanness, its anemic condition, and to posit instead an expansive notion of politics as a serious engagement with normative questions: Whose field of action should be expanded? Whose life chances should be enhanced? Whose voices should be amplified?

While public schools have never lived up to their democratic or transformative potential, they have, until quite recently, been accepted as a public trust and a public good. But today the ideal of public education itself is under attack—not the practice nor the putative failures of the schools, but the very notion that there ought to be free common schools available to all—and that attack comes not from the margins, but from the White House and the other centers of ruling power. The broad framework of that attack targets bureaucracy but not the distribution of educational resources, waste but not inequality. Most disturbing of all, the current attack on public education is openly and explicitly an attack on democracy: the market will be "more efficient" than the polis, they say; competition is "less messy" than participation. We are asked to look inward and not outward, to take care of our own and let other people's children fend for themselves. Our field of vision is narrowed immeasurably as we struggle to defend what we have, or debate agendas that are worthy of neither our spirit nor our imagination.

Democracy in America is too often reduced to slogans and symbols. Democracy, then, is neither an ideal nor a quest, but an object—something we have and the rest of the world covets. Voting in presidential elections is down 20%, and two-thirds of the people believe the government is run by a small, self-interested elite. Deeper and more authentic forms of participation are degraded and destroyed, while the gaudier and more elaborate symbols—the Stars and Stripes, the national anthem, the Statue of Liberty—are put forward more insistently than ever. Pundits tell us that Super Tuesday is an example of political sophistication, while the TV news bombards us with endless variations of a single story: you have random chances of encountering murder and mayhem, and equally random chances of suddenly becoming rich and famous. People are reduced to a faceless mob, a nuisance at best, or small, selfish cliques that menace the rest of us. Work is what we want to avoid, and accomplishment is rarely mentioned. Against these obstacles and more, George Wood has planted his flag.

Our earliest slogan in SDS was "Let the People Decide." That is as good a place as any to continue the struggle and to begin anew.

CHAPTER 6

Ten Ways to Be a Good School

John Taylor Gatto taught in New York City public schools for 26 years, and in 1991 he was selected as New York State's Teacher of the Year. At the awards ceremony—the festival where the happy-face sticker is ritualistically placed on the honoree's chest—Gatto put a pie in the face of the self-congratuatory assembly by saying, in effect, that schools murder the souls and minds of children *by design,* and that he's been fighting a guerrilla war against genocide in the classroom his whole life—a war he is losing badly.

In *Dumbing Us Down: The Hidden Curriculum of Compulsory Schooling* (1992), Gatto's victory speech, along with other occasional writings, is available to a wider audience. Streetwise and blunt, Gatto pulls no punches: "The lesson of report cards, grades, and tests is that children should not trust themselves or their parents but should instead rely on the evaluation of certified officials" (p. 11); "Children will follow a private drummer if you can't get them into a uniformed marching band" (p. 12); "It is the most important lesson, that we must wait for other people, better trained than ourselves, to make the meanings of our lives" (p. 8); "first and foremost [schooling] is a jobs project and an agency for letting contracts" (p. 9).

Gatto outlines in excruciating detail the real lessons of American schooling, things like hierarchy and your place in it, indifference, emotional and intellectual dependency, provisional self-esteem, and the requirement that each of us submit passively to certified authority. The experience of schooling is that nothing of real importance is ever undertaken, nothing is ever connected to anything else, nothing is ever pursued to its deepest limits, nothing is ever finished, and nothing is ever done with investment and courage.

"Children learn what they live," Gatto argues: "Put kids in a class and they will live out their lives in an invisible cage, isolated from their chance at community; interrupt kids with bells and horns

all the time and they will learn that nothing is important; force them
to plead for their natural right to the toilet and they will become
liars and toadies; ridicule them and they will retreat from human
association; shame them and they will find a hundred ways to get
even" (p. 76).

No wonder we produce a recognizably American student who
is, as Gatto quotes Bertrand Russell, "anti-intellectual, supersti-
tious, lacking self-confidence [or] inner freedom . . . [and] inadequate to the personal crises of their lives" (p. 78). Education is bold,
adventurous, creative, vivid, and illuminating. In other words, education is for explorers, thinkers, and citizens. Clearly our schools
have little to do with education. Training is for slaves, for loyal subjects, for tractable employees and good soldiers. Education tears
down walls; training is all barbed wire.

At a gathering of the North Dakota Study Group, an irregular band of guerrilla educators, visions of a better way were everywhere. These are not idle reveries but concrete accounts from the
field, reports grounded in practice and action. The participants were
visionaries and activists, dreamers and doers. The dazzling array of
projects, struggles, organizations, and efforts—hundreds of them—
in itself became, for me, cause for celebration and hope.

My notes from the study group reflect conversations overheard
and engaged in, workshops, presentations, long walks and meals
shared. The words belong to many: Hubert Dyasi, Vito Perrone,
Lillian Weber, Richard Gray, Mercedes Soto, Helen Featherstone,
Eleanor Duckworth, Debbie Meier, and others. So many openings
and possibilities. I thought of John Taylor Gatto and the murder of
children's minds and lives, and the thousands of struggles against all
of this. And in my notes I began to frame sketches of 10 conversations, and from these, 10 characteristics of a good school.

1. *A good school is lived in the present tense.* Teachers provide opportunities for rich experiences and powerful interactions *right
now.* A good teacher assumes that the best preparation for a meaningful future life lies in creating a meaningful present life. The
work of school is not constructed as bitter medicine, hurriedly
swallowed on someone else's promise that it will be profitable for
you "someday." In fact, "preparation" is not the best way to frame

issues of teaching and learning, and so preparation is bracketed and our work is never justified by reference to it.

The work of the school is learning, and learning (like living) is its own justification—it must be infused with urgency and immediacy. While it is often improvisational, ragged, and uneven, it must be relevant in its own right. Attending to matters of importance, pursuing issues of interest and concern, finding useful work to do—these become the benchmarks of good practice.

2. *A good school is a workshop for inventors.* Children are human beings (not assets or cargo, not human becomings), and human beings are by nature inventors. Of course, some of us invent famous machines or technologies or institutions, but all of us create works as expressions of our consciousness. The young child learning to speak, the older child working at the easel and discovering the color purple through that work, the class inquiring into employment and neighborhood housing and finding patterns based on race—these are all examples of inventors at work. Since everything is on some level a human invention—literature and the arts, math and science, and also racism, sexism, even childhood itself—a good school is one in which people are expected and encouraged to be inventors, and where we explore together consequences of human inventions both for the growth of children and for the society we want to build.

3. *A good school is fearless.* It is safe, yes—both physically and emotionally, because we know that fear destroys intelligence—but also designed for risk-taking. It is a place that discourages *acquiescence,* the passive dullness that is the hallmark of most schools, in favor of building collective *consent.* Teachers here believe that while you can have compulsory schooling, compulsory education is an unworkable contradiction. Education and learning require assent, some personal act of courage and will and affirmation. And so teachers struggle to construct a place where matters of paramount importance are developed and pursued in a compelling way, a place that draws students' interest, attention, and consistent presence on its own basis.

4. *A good school honors diversity.* While diversity has many dimensions, consider race as a central example. In a good school race and racial differences are not the basis for privilege and op-

pression, but neither are they ignored or dismissed. Rather, race, racial differences, and racism as both bias and structural form are explored and studied. They are studied because these constructions have defined so much of our own history, and continue to motivate and power human thinking and action today.

The assumption in this school is that racism hurts all people and is a force that can degrade education and stunt growth; that stratification along racial lines blocks progress and the fulfillment of potential; and that simply because grown-ups can't talk or work sensibly around issues of race is no reason it can't be a schoolwide focus of inquiry and action. To the extent that this focus draws people of different races together in a common cause, the school also attends to internal questions: What expectations do we have of one another? How do we work in a way that acknowledges and respects the contributions of each? What are the formal and informal "rules of the house," and who decides what they are? How do we create a productive tension between comfort and discomfort in our process and in our study?

5. *In a good school there are high expectations and standards for all.* In this school standards are not reduced to immutable laws or mindless benchmarks for testing, but are principles and values around which to reflect and raise questions. In fact, standard-setting is part of the conscious, stipulated work of the school. Standards are developed close to the classroom, by the students and the teacher, and close to the family, by the child and the parents. They are not held outside or above the concerns of those most intimately involved in the growth and development of children, and therefore they are not thoughtless, lifeless, or disfiguring.

A core question, one that is dynamic, ever-changing, and alive for each person, that guides much of the work of a good school, is this: What knowledge and experience are most worthwhile? In this school we acknowledge the human impulse to value and to express preferences, and we treat values as if they matter.

6. *In a good school adults tell children the truth.* Most schools live on half-truths and lies, and dissembling is the sad, often exhausting norm of behavior. One pervasive example is the notion that standardized test scores are a fair measure of student intelligence, achievement, or worth.

This is not true. Think what would happen if students were told that the single most powerful predictor of academic success, including scores on those tests, is family income and class background. Furthermore, think what would happen if students were told that the scoring of tests is structured so that half of all test-takers must fail. Suddenly the all-powerful Oz would be revealed for the old fraud that he is. This could lead to a range of interesting investigations, projects, and activities—all based on simply pushing back the hidden screen and looking at who's pulling the strings.

7. *A good school is an intimate community where children find unconditional acceptance.* In many schools nothing about children—not their lives or experiences, nor their families or communities—is deemed valuable. Their very presence is seen as a burden, and is always contingent: they are sorted, classified, graded, moved along. By contrast, a good school is a place where students feel they have a right and a responsibility to be present, a place that could not function without the contribution of each particular kid. This becomes the touchstone for trust and hope.

8. *A good school is a thoughtful place that honors the thinking and the work of teachers and students.* It is also a place that consciously provides opportunities for the community to enact its values: compassion, perhaps, or curiosity, justice, openness, humor, creativity. In this school we have resisted the pressure to push out all that is most important and worthwhile in learning and living in favor of a narrow, instructable, and easily testable agenda. Rather, we have created the conditions to experience and enact our values, and have struggled to recover a language of valuing that had been weakened through disuse.

9. *A good school is simple, dark, and deep.* It is a place where big questions can be followed to their outer limits because the pressure to "cover the curriculum" is pushed back, and the pretense of coverage is rejected. It is a place that encourages curiosity and engages mystery.

10. *A good school is a place where people make a difference.* Citizenship is considered a practical art here, and it is therefore practiced rather than ritualized. Students struggle to extract knowledge from information, to consider the common good, and to link consciousness to conduct. Classrooms in this school are characterized

by activity, discovery, and surprise rather than passivity and rote repetition.

A good school stands in critical opposition to the schooling we see all around us. Based on a different vision of human life and potential, such a school is a radical alternative. And radical alternatives are desperately needed—for the lives of our children now and for the hope of creating a new social order.

PART II

TEACHING IN TODAY'S SCHOOLS

No classroom or school can ever be child-centered if it doesn't struggle to become family-centered and community-centered. Children's lives are embedded, and if everything about their communities and families is constructed as an obstacle, an encumbrance, a deficit, there is simply no basis for an education of hope and freedom. Teachers must find ways to map the assets not only of their students, but of the relationships and contexts that surround them.

Teachers make hundreds of choices every day, and those choices have powerful reverberations in the choices students will make today and tomorrow. This is why teachers must struggle to become more aware, more thoughtful, more caring, more connected.

Good teaching is not automatic; it is always a struggle. It is filled with initiative and risk, but also with satisfaction and joy. It is intricate, complex, deep, and wide. It is never twice the same.

This section asks you to think about teaching in today's schools as equal parts gift and challenge. It assumes that whatever constraints and limits are placed on teachers, there are always openings in which to enact something new. It asks teachers to choose for themselves and for their students.

CHAPTER 7

Teaching City Kids

with Therese Quinn

Direct instruction is marching its way to the front of the class. Drills and more drills conducted with a regimented, military precision promise to create an unquestioning, obedient workforce, a compliant citizenry. The message: Don't think, just do it. Do only what you're told, of course. Perfect training for other people's children—training to be in line and on time, training in mindless repetition, boredom, and irrelevance. Chain gangs are making a comeback, prison construction is a growth industry—Bantu education in American cities suddenly fits and reflects the times we're enduring.

Martin Haberman, in a thin but powerful book called *Star Teachers of Children in Poverty* (1995), offers a refreshing alternative: an education of power for children of the poor. Haberman—tough, streetwise, straight-talking, unmistakably urban—has been there, and he knows what it takes for teachers to work effectively with children in poverty. For years his research and advocacy have focused on the ways city schools cheat children of the urban poor out of an education of value, and what we might do about it. Here Haberman offers a useful guide to teachers who strive to make a difference.

Haberman begins by describing what good teachers don't do. Importantly, they are not obsessed with control. They don't spend much time worrying about discipline. They don't have many rules. They never "get physical" with punishment. They don't use behavior modification techniques to "trick" their students into doing work. Haberman notes that most of this runs counter to what many teachers believe and implement, and what many teacher education programs teach.

So what do these "good" teachers do? Something simple but

radical in our typically depersonalizing educational bureaucracies: they place each child at the center of a learning orbit. They pay exquisite attention to each child, and they turn each child's interests and strengths into projects which open opportunities for success. In other words, star teachers find ways to let their students shine. And then these teachers don't give up. The heart of it is simple: kids can learn, and every teacher's job is to find out how to turn them on to learning. Of course problems happen, these teachers say, and it's part of the job to deal with them, but problems aren't the focus. People are.

Haberman also makes it clear that no amount of emphasis on "in the future" jobs, test scores, or other external rewards will initiate or substitute for the real and lasting motivation that comes from loving learning. He asks: how can a teacher teach a love of learning when they don't model the naturalness and pleasure of learning and thinking every day in the classroom? Curiosities and intellectual passions are necessarily idiosyncratic, and can't be taught through mindless direct instruction drills, or assessed through worksheets. To lead a child to joyful reading, a teacher must love literature, not merely know the alphabet. And the new reader should learn the power of reading, writing words that matter, not drills and chants isolated from meaning.

Haberman's passion and anger are muted throughout the first two chapters. But in the third he lets it roll. The key is here: belief must be linked to behavior. Passion and politics. Without an ideological underpinning, Haberman insists, teachers will just be going through the motions, sometimes right, sometimes wrong, but always without guidelines. Fine for the teachers, but for children in poverty, school success is crucial. He spells it out: children in poverty start with the least, and then they tend to get the worst. And this is not a benign process, not a simple lack that can be compensated for later; school failure can mean, probably will mean, life failure for many of these children. At a minimum, it will mean several reduced life chances.

Haberman is obviously consumed with the urgency of his tasks, to right, right now, the dreadful conditions that stifle the learning lives of many of this nation's young. He writes, "Our society accepts and supports an educational system that is ostensibly fair in its competition but inevitably produces winners and losers. The only issue that seems to remain is how to educate happy compliant losers rather than anti-social ones" (1995, p. 61). This is a powerful indictment of education, and it is the heart of his beef with failing teachers: they are the enforcers, however unwittingly, of this terrible, child-blighting system, a system that was never intended to work for these children, and indisputably doesn't. He warns that good teachers will face opposition, probably frequently, as they try to teach "around" the established curriculum and methods in their schools.

Haberman approvingly mentions teachers who cut their intercom wires and ignore all central office paperwork. He implies that teachers will need to subvert the system to be effective. He also implies a need to protect urban students from the hopelessness that might result from really understanding the system they are stuck in. Perhaps in this he underestimates urban children and their parents. Most urban children know that teachers and school systems don't always have their best interests in mind, just as they have been taught that the police aren't always their friends. That's realistic, and protective. A teacher who understands this, and addresses it honestly, can help her students maneuver toward success. Yes, the nation could do with less hopelessness, cynicism, and griping, but we certainly need more people who can critique and are willing to take action. Joe Hill's advice, "Don't mourn, organize," seems apt.

Haberman constantly redirects the reader's attention to the children themselves—he gives clear and practical tips on everything from assigning homework to using classroom computers. And more important, Haberman demands that teachers be thoughtful and courageous. He reminds us that "compulsive rule-following" is a pitfall of bureaucracy and schools, and warns us against it. This is a start. We need to follow the implications toward encouraging teachers to have, teach, and model a proactive kind of "civic courage," a quality that will not only help them build more successful, democratic classrooms, but will also show students how they, too, can build a more just future for us all.

CHAPTER 8

Sometimes a Shining Moment

Foxfire is "an organism that grows on decaying organic matter in damp, dark caves in the mountains and glows in the dark." The high school students in Eliot Wiggington's class who voted to call their fledgling magazine *Foxfire* decades ago probably had no idea that their project would soon take the nation by storm, popularizing the details of Appalachian culture, propelling their fantastic and mysterious name into the American idiom, and spinning off, among other things, a series of bestselling books, a string band, a record company, a press, a cable television channel, a folklore museum, and a Broadway play. But given the keen sense of humor and intelligence that many teenagers possess, some may well have had in mind a metaphor for students, or for that matter, for the entire enterprise of schooling when they settled on the name *Foxfire:* decaying organic matter that can shine in surprising ways. In any case, it remains a fitting and inventive image, critical without being cynical, hopeful and yet ironic.

Sometimes a Shining Moment (Wiggington, 1988) is the story of the Foxfire experience, and the autobiography of the outstanding teacher who shaped and shepherded that project from the start. This is a fine book—thoughtful, visionary, and immensely useful. It is useful in at least two senses: first, teachers, policymakers, and students of education will find Wiggington's narrative and the philosophical musings that flow from his experience provocative, challenging, and in many cases empowering; second, practicing teachers will welcome the resource materials in the bibliography, including course guides, a detailed description of a model grammar and composition course, and suggestions for developing courses that can do double duty—that is, courses that can meet state and district requirements even as they serve higher philosophical and pedagogical goals.

Eliot Wiggington graduated from Cornell and began teaching high school in 1966 with an unpolished but sincere ideal of serving others. He chose Rabun Gap, Georgia, because it was situated near his childhood home in a part of the world where he wanted to settle. His account of his first year teaching in the Rabun Gap-Nacoochee School will be painfully familiar to anyone who has stood in front of a group of children and presumed to teach them anything:

> I had never been in a situation before where I was so completely confused by all that was going on around me . . . It was a through-the-looking-glass world where the friendlier I was . . . the more liberties the students took and the harder it became to accomplish anything . . . I'd crack down . . . and the mood would turn sullen and resentful and no sharing and learning would take place . . . It was impossible. I began to regard them collectively as the enemy and I became the prisoner . . . (Wiggington, 1988, p. 31)

On one particular gloomy morning Wiggington confessed to his students his own disappointment and admitted the obvious: his classes were a failure both for him and for them. He asked them what they thought they could do together in order to make it through the year. The honesty of the question and the candor of its presentation broke the pattern of failure. After hesitation and awkward beginnings, a conversation began.

Wiggington resisted falling back into conventional teaching habits and let this newly found authentic dialogue guide him in the curriculum and style of his teaching. The conversation grew and developed, spinning off project ideas, readings, and assignments along the way. He asked students to write a composition describing positive or negative school experiences that stood out in their minds. The students' responses awakened his own childhood memories of school, and his personal list of positive experiences included times when visitors from the outside world brought interesting and engaging projects into the classroom, times when the students were given genuine responsibility, and times when their work was projected beyond the classroom to a larger audience.

Wiggington was becoming a student of teaching, a researcher into the lives of his students, and, as is the case in all true dialogues, he had to become an acute listener as well as a speaker. One day a

student—"one of my sixth-period losers" (1988, p. 69)—said he'd
be out of class for a few days because he was going into the woods
to collect "sang" for a "sang bed." Curious and fascinated, Wiggington asked if he could go along during his free time. The experience
taught Wiggington more than he imagined there was to know about
ginseng, and more importantly, it transformed his relationship with
his "sixth-period loser" into one of mutual respect and deeper understanding. He learned that dialogue demanded that students become the authors of their own experiences. He found that when
their lives were treated with respect, students responded with respect, and when engaged in work that they thought to be of value,
they treated it valuably. *Foxfire*, initially conceived of as a literary
magazine, became a journal of culture and history, a magazine filled
with students' projects and interests, photographs, interviews, and
essays on the lives of their own relatives and neighbors. It was simultaneously an affirmation of the students' lives and heritage, and
an active search for their own authentic voices.

As *Foxfire* expanded from an extracurricular journal to become
the central focus of his classroom work, Wiggington discovered his
own pathway to authentic teaching, including his admirable composition course. Cynics might argue that Wiggington's teaching style
worked for him because of the extraordinary person he is, and that
only a superhuman could accomplish what he did in the classroom.
The criticism begs the question. Before there was a magazine, a book,
recognition, and rewards, there was a confused and despairing young
teacher in a high school classroom. What he did then can be done
by most teachers now. Instead of working as junior management
and imposing a culture of competition and conformity on students,
teachers everywhere can discover ways to validate the dignity and
worth of students. *Foxfire* is one model of choosing for students.

Foxfire has inspired a host of similar projects around the country. There is a moving account of an exchange between Wiggington's
poor white Appalachian kids and a group of primarily Puerto Rican
kids on New York City's Lower East Side who developed a magazine
called *The Fourth Street*. The students from New York City and Georgia, developing a sense of the worth of their own cultures, became
open to the worth of others as well.

Wiggington promotes and endorses the development of other
"Foxfires," but he resists imposing form or content. He describes, for

example, a "white teacher of Indian children insisting that they all start a magazine like *Foxfire,* only to discover that the culture forbids the writing down and sharing of many cultural customs with the outside world."

Wiggington's story has parallels in the autobiographical narratives of other teachers. In *36 Children,* Herb Kohl (1988) describes the sense of unreality he experienced as he assigned his first homework and realized that the "words weighed heavy and false; it wasn't my voice but some common tyrant" (p. 9). Kohl's search for authenticity led him to an autobiographical writing project with students in which they wrote about their blocks and their lives in Harlem. Kohl became a valuable resource, facilitator, reader, editor, and critic for them, and was also inspired by their honesty and courage to complete a difficult writing project of his own.

Sylvia Ashton-Warner, author of *Teacher* and *Spinster,* based her "organic teaching" of reading on a deep respect for the richness and authenticity of the lives and language of her young Maori students in New Zealand. In her "infant room" youngsters authored their own stories, spoke with their own voices, and revealed their own truths. Her unpublished Maori storybooks must have looked a lot like *Foxfire.*

It is true that no teacher is a perfectly free agent. Wiggington began *Foxfire* at a time when there was arguably more support for innovation in education than there is today. The civil rights and antiwar movements were shaking society to its core, and change and experimentation were in the air. Progressive social movements changed human expectations and social relations, creating an environment of expanded possibility.

Furthermore, the very strength of *Foxfire,* explicitly bringing students' lives into their schoolwork, must carry along the contradictions of their lives as well, the oppressiveness, for example, or the narrow thinking. On this score, one wishes Wiggington had discussed the impact of racism on his work—perhaps its absence highlights the point that Wiggington is not a "superteacher," but rather an individual like the rest of us, shaped by and teaching amidst powerful social and economic forces, forces that coerce and constrain, prod and bombard, push and pull, forces that can also expand options and open possibilities. Teachers are constrained by their relationship to power and their roles in reproducing social relations, and we can find ourselves accomplices in a corrupt undertaking. But we are not merely that.

While powerful forces in society might have heavy, intricate designs on schools, these designs must filter, after all, through the work of teachers. When the classroom door is closed and the noise from outside and inside has settled, a teacher chooses. She can decide to satisfy distant demands or not, accommodate established expectations or not, embrace her own narrowest self-interest or not. She can decide whether to merely survive another day of inexhaustible demands and limited energy. Or she can decide, for example, to interpret and invent, to resist and rebel.

The sad thing, of course, is that teaching based on dialogue, respect, and empowerment remains as revolutionary, untried, and despised by the educational establishment today as ever. And now, more than ever, such teaching is needed. Herb Kohl said it this way:

> The time of greatest need for children to be cared for and well educated is during a time of neglect. It is wonderful to be teaching in the midst of a social movement like the civil rights movement, as I did at the beginning of my career. But it is much more important now, when society is indifferent and hope for a decent future for all children is considered romantic and even foolish. The loneliness of trying to teach well during cynical times also promises rewards. Young people and their parents know who cares, and there is a warmth and a sense of common struggle that comes from caring when it's easy to be cynical. And the children themselves can come alive and their minds unfold because of one teacher . . . You can see and feel your students grow, and that finally is the reason to teach and the reward of teaching. (1988, p. 163)

Eliot Wiggington echoes these sentiments. Foxfire. Out of the mountain caves something is glowing in the dark. Something alive.

CHAPTER 9

Learning from Children

Our youngest child came into our family when he was 14 months old—unexpected, unannounced. Chesa was set adrift when his biological parents could no longer care for him and after a short stay with his grandparents, he came to us.

For a long time he was an easy child—agreeable, eager to please, perhaps a bit compliant. He was never fussy, never demanding. On the other side, he never displayed much enthusiasm: his play lacked commitment and his explorations of the world were tentative. He watched his new brothers at play—one almost four years older, the other just a half-year older—but he joined in rather reluctantly. Subject to every sore throat and ear infection that came along, his physical strength and his emotions seemed to be ever at a low ebb. He was downcast, depressed. Later his depression gave way to an explosive anger, often self-directed. He was clumsy both physically and socially, and he would frequently crash into people and things—sometimes hurting himself and often angering others—and then genuinely wonder what had happened.

Chesa also had qualities that could help him negotiate and take control of his life. One was his dogged determination—his willingness to work and work and work at a task or a challenge until he succeeded. When his mind was set, he never gave up and he never gave in, no matter what. Another quality was his keen intelligence and his steel-trap memory. His telling of events or conversations was filled with color and nuance, detail and particulars. Finally, he could be incredibly compassionate and unexpectedly generous. Each of these, of course, could be experienced two ways: his iron will could be seen as stubbornness or resoluteness, his memory as acute or obsessive, his sweetness as strong or weak. As he set off for first grade, we were painfully aware of the two-sided way Chesa might be experienced. There was the matter of anger and temper, for example, and the highly visible issue of plowing into people. Who would his teacher see coming through the door? How would she know our wonderful child?

We were lucky: Chesa's teacher, a young man named Kevin Sweeney, admired his strengths and quickly figured out interesting and clever ways to leverage these against his weaknesses. For example, he gave Chesa cleaning tasks almost every day, not the routine classroom stuff, but tasks that tapped into his workhorse nature: "Chesa, could you wash these shelves this afternoon? Just move the paper over here and then use a bucket of soapy water and a sponge." This not only focused Chesa on a goal, but it made a worthwhile quality more visible to himself and to the other children, and this, in turn, made him a stronger, more accepted group member. Furthermore, it provided the teacher with a steady reminder of something to value in Chesa, who was a challenging child for much of the day.

All of this came back to me when I was working with a group of 10-year-old boys in an inner-city public school. I showed them a simple structure for writing a brief autobiographical sketch or poem. The first line is your first name, followed by a line of three words that describe you to yourself. The next line is something you love, then something you hate, something you fear, and something you wish for. The last line is your last name. I gave the kids this example:

> I am Martin
> courageous non-violent warrior
> I love all people
> I hate oppression
> I am afraid of ignorance
> I wish for freedom
> King

Hannibal pointed our that I had left out "Luther," which was right, so we made the last line, "Luther King." They then made poems for themselves:

> I am Hannibal
> fluky but funny
> I love the Bulls

I hate being whipped
I am afraid of Freddy
I wish for Michael Jordan to come over
Johnson.

I am Aaron
small, black, frightened
I love my mom
I hate being picked on
I am afraid of the raper man and the police
I wish for happiness
Blackwell.

When I had asked his teacher if Aaron could join me for an hour that morning, as he had on other occasions, she had practically pushed him out the door. "He's no good today," she had said. "His mind is wandering and he doesn't want to work." I looked at Aaron again. He was small, frail really, and he did look frightened. He smiled a lot, but always apologetically, looking down, unsure. He was quiet, never initiating talk or play, always reacting. His face was streaked, his hair uncombed, and his eyes were puffy and resting on large dark circles. Even in the company of other poor children, Aaron looked down and out. I wondered: Why is Aaron frightened? Who are the police in his life? What is this happiness he wishes for?

As we talked about his poem, I learned that the "raper man" was a large character in his life, someone Aaron could describe physically even though he'd never actually seen him. He had huge hands and was ugly, with big red bumps on his face. He drove an old, wrecked car. He was often sighted by other children on the walk from school to home, so Aaron and his little sister mainly ran home each day. The police loomed large: while he didn't know any himself, two of his brothers had had frequent encounters with the law. Aaron told me a long story of one brother, James, who had been falsely accused of gang membership and was arrested in a playground "for just being there." Aaron had visited James yesterday in Cook County Jail, he told me, and today James would go on trial for first-degree murder. "My mom says maybe he'll come home this week if the judge sees he didn't do it."

I think back to his teacher's comment. "He's no good today. His mind is wandering and he doesn't want to work." I wonder if I'd be any good with my brother on trial for murder, or if I could concentrate on worksheets with all this going on. Then I think of his mother, and I wonder what her hopes are for Aaron in school. I think of her in light of our hopes for Chesa, and our good fortune in having him known and understood by Kevin. What could she tell his teacher about Aaron that would be of use? Would the teacher or anyone else in the school care? Would they find a way to teach him?

When teachers look out over their classrooms, what do they see? Half-civilized barbarians? Savages? A collection of deficits or IQs or averages? Little banks to be filled with our daily deposits? Do they see fellow creatures? We see students in our classrooms, of course, but do we really observe them? Who do we see? What dreams do they bring? What experiences have they had, and where do they want to go? What interests or concerns them, how have they been hurt, what are they frightened of, what will they fight for, and what and whom do they care about?

When I first taught, we were told that many of our students were "culturally deprived." This became a strong, germinal idea for some teachers, and cultural deprivation was being unearthed and remediated all over the place. It didn't take long, however, for cultural deprivation as a concept to come in for some serious and sustained questioning: Is calling someone "culturally deprived" the same as calling them not-white, not-middle-class? Is Spanish a "lower" language than English? Is the implication that some cultures are superior and others inferior? Or that some children have a culture and others do not? What is culture, anyway? In time the concept of cultural deprivation was discredited as patronizing and untrue, and it fell into disuse.

Unhappily, labeling students has become a toxic habit in the intervening years—it is an all-out epidemic in our schools. It's as if supervisors, coordinators, and administrators have nothing better to do than to mumble knowingly about "soft signs," "attention deficit disorder," or "low impulse control," and all the rest of us stand around smiling, pretending to know what they're talking about. The categories keep splintering and proliferating, getting nuttier as they go: LD, BD, EH, TAG, EMH. It's almost impossible for teachers today not to see before them "gifted and talented" students, "learning disabled" youngsters, and children "at risk." I once asked a scholar who had just presented a major research paper at a professional conference on "at-risk" students to give me a brief definition of at-risk, using only "Peter Rabbit English." He said flatly, "Black or Hispanic, poor, and from a single-parent household." YIPES! "At risk" is simply "cultural deprivation" recycled for modern times.

The problem is this: in the human-centered act of teaching, all attempts to fit kids into categories lower our sights, misdirect our vision, and mislead our intentions. Labels are limiting. They offer a single lens concentrated on a specific deficit when what we need are multiple ways of seeing a child's ever-changing strengths. All the categories are upside-down—they conceal more than they reveal. They are abstract, when what we need is immediate and concrete. The focusing questions for effective teachers must be these: Who is this person before me? What are his interests and areas of wonder? How does she express herself, and what is her awareness of herself as a learner? What efforts and potential does she bring? These are the kinds of questions we need to attend to.

In the odd, often upside-down world of schools, we typically start in the wrong place. We start with what kids can't do and don't know, what they don't understand or value, what they feel incompetent or insecure about, and we then develop a curriculum to remediate each deficiency. The deficit-model curriculum is built on repairing weakness. And it simply doesn't work.

Frederick Douglass tells a remarkable story of learning to read as a subversive activity. As a slave Douglass had no rights and meager opportunities. Reading among slaves was strictly forbidden, for it could open worlds and create unimaginable mischief. Besides, slaves had no need for reading. They could be trained in the necessary menial and backbreaking work. Yet his master's wife, believing him to be an intelligent youngster, undertook to teach Douglass how to read the Bible in hopes that he would come closer to God. When the master discovered the crime he exploded: "It will unfit him to be a slave!"

Education will unfit anyone to be a slave. That is because education is bold, adventurous, creative, vivid, illuminating—in other words, education is for self-activating explorers of life, for those who would challenge fate, for doers and activists, for citizens. Training is for slaves, for loyal subjects, for tractable employees, for willing consumers, for obedient soldiers. Education tears down walls; training is all barbed wire.

What we call education is usually no more than training. We are often so busy operating schools that we have lost sight of learning. We mostly participate in certification mills, institutions founded on notions of control and discipline, lifeless and joyless places where people serve time and master a few basic skills on their way to a plain piece of paper that justifies and sanctions the whole business. Sometimes these places are merely mindless, and sometimes they are expressly malevolent.

A hundred years ago this country developed a system of schools run by the Interior Department called Indian boarding schools, a few of which survive to this day. The premise of these schools was that Native American children must be stripped of everything Indian and taught to be like whites. Taken from their homes, these youngsters were punished severely for speaking their own languages, practicing their own religions, or attempting to contact their families. Everything Native had to be erased as a first step toward official learning. Some students, of course, went along, but many rebelled, refused to learn, and were labeled intractable.

The cost of education at an Indian boarding school was huge—dignity, identity, one's full humanity, sometimes even sanity. The payoff was rather small: a menial job and a marginal place. Students had to submit to humiliation, degradation, and mutilation simply to earn a place on the lowest rung of the social order. No wonder most refused: the price was high, the benefit meager.

It is not much different in too many schools today. We claim to be giving students key skills and knowledge, and yet we deny them the one thing that is essential to their survival: something to live for. All the curriculum units together—whether in drug awareness, gang prevention, mental health, or literature and history—are not worth that single, simple, expectant thing.

CHAPTER 10

"We'll Have Great Fun If It Stops Raining": Reflections on Seventh-Grade Camp

Hello mudda,
Hello fadda,
Here I am at
Camp Granada.
Camp is very
Entertaining.
And they say we'll have great fun
If it stops raining.
—Allan Sherman

In the spring of 1990 I was invited by the middle school faculty to join them as a group leader at 7th-grade camp. I would supervise, sleep out, cook over an open fire, and live in the woods for three days with a dozen or so 12- and 13-year-olds at an adventure center in Michigan. Sounded like heaven. I was the only parent invited to go, and I was honored, even touched. Zayd, our 7th-grader, wore that wonderfully adolescent look of self-conscious horror combined with bursting pride. "I can't be in your group," he told me with what sounded like disappointment. "But try not to do anything embarrassing." A tall order for me, in Zayd's mind.

A few days after details of the trip were sent to parents, I ran into a father at a 7th-grade play who slapped me hard on the back and with a patronizing smile, his voice dripping with sarcasm, said, "Lucky you!" "Lucky me," I replied weakly. However, as a teacher educator, my background gave me all the equipment I needed—I hoped.

In our culture, "adolescence" is constructed as problematic at best. Teenagers are trouble. If you don't believe it, consult anyone who's raised one. Talk to a friend. Check with your own parents. Ask preadolescents or teens themselves—they are painfully aware of the stereotypes and clichés, and worry about what's going on. Or remember how many times acquaintances and even perfect strangers have told you teenage horror stories, or cruelly kidded you about what awaits your family when the dreaded teen years descend.

The enduring themes from popular culture play out perfectly in the horror classic *I Was a Teenage Werewolf,* and the real-life variations are perfectly scripted: this sweet young child who never did anything wrong in life is transformed into a snarling beast driven by animal impulses. The kid is some inexplicable mutant with out-of-control hormones and wild, insane desires. The eruption of hair—especially hair—where there was once smooth and delicate skin is the physical signal that the nightmare is about to begin: the teenager is consumed with a self-loathing that turns to rage, and everyone else had better get out of the way. If you cross this creature, you're dead.

We might agree that the transition from childhood to adulthood is not all sweetness and light, that the turmoil has a strong physical basis and some real cultural power. But there are alternative ways of looking at this particular passage, and we need not be total victims of a B-movie plot—we can try to write our own scripts.

One place to begin is to revisit a concept popular in early childhood but strangely absent here: "developmentally appropriate." Put simply, we might consider the environment, activities, and opportunities for experiences that are likely to nurture and challenge human beings at specific points in their growth and development. For middle schoolers the questions would include: What are adolescents like? What are their compelling developmental needs and tasks? How can we define their developmental tasks? What would constitute a successful passage through these years? What kinds of experiences would likely help youngsters at this stage?

These are complex questions, to be sure, and to engage them requires some serious thought. Briefly (and inadequately), adolescence is certainly a time of dramatic change, a time when human beings say good-bye to childhood and enter the adult world. The onset of puberty with its rapid and dramatic physical changes is the tip of the iceberg. Adolescents also experience a qualitative change in cognitive development: they begin to think seriously about their own thinking and the thinking of others, and they are now capable of sustained abstract reasoning. They are intensely curious and often idealistic, willing to work hard on projects that interest and engage them.

They are swept with further emotional and social changes as they struggle to broaden the base of affiliation beyond their families and into a wider circle of friends. Society and the crowd become a focus of huge concern. As when they passed from baby to child 10 years before, adolescents are opening to a new sense of identity, and a new way of seeing and participating in the world. And as before, there is turmoil, some sadness, and a bit of upheaval and confusion, as every "yes" requires a corresponding "no." Adolescence is a time of grieving as well as celebration, of saying good-bye to the safety and comfort of childhood, and hello to the rest of your life. Of course, now they inhabit huge, crashing bodies, and they often feel as misunderstood and clumsy as Edward Scissorhands or Spider-man. The challenge for the adults in their lives, as before, is to figure out how to hold on to the young children they are, and how to let go when they are capable of flying free.

Let me return to 7th-grade camp. Who would have thought there would be constant snow, sleet, and freezing rain from May 9 to May 11 in lower Michigan? That's exactly what happened. The planned physical challenge of the Outward Bound–type ropes course paled in comparison to the spontaneous challenge to stay dry and warm. Everyone has tales to tell; my own personal hell included failing to bring everything on the list of suggested items (a change of shoes, for example) and having undergone (one day before camp) a middle-aged rite of passage—gum surgery. So while I froze, spit blood, and took painkillers, others froze, had water fights, and argued over whose turn it was to get more firewood.

It rained and rained. We attacked the ropes course and survived. And it rained. Kids contemplated the importance of teamwork after scaling a wall together, and considered the value of partnership as they leaned on one another to avoid falling off the high ropes. We learned a lot, ate bad food, adjusted to the outhouse. And it rained. The camp staff became defensive, apologetic, and even broke one of their cardinal rules: they took all our stuff off and dried it. When a staff person returned clothes and sleeping bags to our campsite, one youngster, apparently accustomed to nothing less, thanked him cursorily and handed him a new batch of wet things with a comment: "Please try to have these done by morning." The staffer rolled his eyes in disbelief.

I enjoyed camp enormously. I loved being with the kids and experiencing up close a group of energetic, engaging, curious, wild, and strange people. I loved the faculty who were there—their concern for the kids and their delight in each accomplishment were an absolute pleasure. I felt fortunate to know that Zayd was spending a year with this group of thoughtful and caring adults.

But camp was too brief. It wasn't long enough for a real rhythm to develop, for a sense of deep accomplishment or growth to occur. Most kids endured it, tolerated it, but never fully engaged in what was possible there. This was our failing, not theirs. In many ways camp was a separate event, something with only tentative links to anything that came before or after. For example, camp was a place potentially to think about groups, how they form and are built, why, and what strengths and weaknesses groups offer. Why is this a concern for only three days at the very end of the school year? Aren't groups and group behavior and the power of the crowd the very center of 7th-grade concerns? Shouldn't this be an ongoing discussion, a centerpiece of the curriculum?

Similarly, camp was a place to consider the value of cooperation. If this is important, why aren't cooperative activity and collective participation structured into all aspects of school life? It's a bit like buying a cooperative learning curriculum package that is used for an hour a day; the rest of the time it's dog-eat-dog.

Camp highlighted for me the things that ought to be a part of every day in school. School could be a place of ongoing challenge, a place where there is real work to do in the context of a cooperative and caring community. School could be a place where youngsters are active and teachers share the adventure of discovery as co-learners, coaches, and guides. School could be a place where students' genuine concerns are discussed and engaged by thoughtful adults, where interests are pursued, every connection followed, and every question opened to a hundred new ones.

All of this, if taken seriously, would mean rethinking much of the machinery of schooling, possibly even throwing out the curriculum as we now conceive it. In its place we might create groups of adults and youngsters who would stay active with one another and alive to asking and re-asking what knowledge and experiences are most worthwhile for our lives and for the lives of others. It might mean, as one teacher remarked to me at the end of camp, giving kids the time, space, and tools to explore the meaning of their own education.

CHAPTER 11

To the Bone:
Reflections in Black and White

A child's question: I am riding an early-morning bus in New York City with Zayd, five years old and just beginning to read. The bus is packed with commuters, the mood a resigned gray grumpiness. Only Zayd is bright-eyed and chirpy as we groan down the avenue toward school and work. "Poppy," Zayd says in his large outside voice, turning to me expectantly. "What's a kike?" A hush seems to fall as 200 eyes lift and, in the sudden silence, begin to sizzle, laser-like, into my head.

What?

"A kike. What's a kike?"

I freeze. I seize up. I buy time: "Where did you hear that word, Zayd?"

"I read it," he replies proudly. "See?" He points to a stab of red graffiti slased across a rear window. "I HATE KIKES," it reads—all upper case—and it is punctuated with a swastika.

"A kike . . ." I stammer. "A kike . . ." I search my erratic mind. I pursue my elusive courage. And then, miraculously, the crowd recedes, and there is only Zayd with his basic trust intact, his childish hope undiminished, alive, his deeply human sense-making engine firing on all cylinders, and I know I must respond simply but honestly, for his sake and for my own.

"Kike," I begin in a clear voice, "is a word full of hatred. It's a word full of violence, a word used by people who want to hurt Jews, like the word 'nigger' is meant to hurt black people. It's a lying word, because it says that some people are more human than others, that some groups are superior to others, that some are less than human. Some people, filled up with hate, might call you a 'kike.' It's

the kind of word we should never use, the kind of word we must always object to and oppose."

Zayd's face never loses its open and intent concentration. "Okay,"
he says simply. "Should you cross it out?"

What a thought! Haven't I done enough? I drag a magic marker
reluctantly from my backpack, walk over, and obliterate the stain.
"Okay," he says again as I turn to face a smiling crowd, a few thumbs-
ups, and an audible collective sigh. I feel—suddenly—better.

A child's questions: Why is the floor sticky? Why is the sky blue?
Why do balls bounce? Why is that man sleeping in the street? Why
is that woman bleeding? Why is my skin brown? A child's questions
innocently ask us to reconsider the world, to confront our own gaps
and ignorances, to rethink the taken-for-granted, the habitual, our
insistent common sense. Their questions can be disruptive and dis-
quieting, to be sure, which may explain the knee-jerk answers we
hear ourselves repeating: I'll tell you later, or when you're older, or
when I have more time, or don't ask, or on and on and on. Our
avoidance reveals our incomprehension, perhaps, but also the fierce
embrace of our personal dogmas, our easy beliefs. And it brings
us face to face with our own temerity—it is frightening, after all, to
open every door, to doubt every truth, to wonder again at every
mystery. "I'll tell you later"—the door slams shut and we sigh with
relief as the illusion of safety descends.

Children's questions can, on the other hand, shock us into new
awarenesses—if we will accede a little. The ground shifts and we are
forced (or invited) to make sense again of all that is before us, to dig
deeper perhaps, to discover something truer, more layered, more
nuanced, more complex. If we take their questions in this way, they
may become occasions for the ethical to emerge. We begin to notice
the obstacles blocking the paths of human beings toward freedom,
toward fulfillment and wholeness in their humanness, and we
wonder how to name those obstacles, how to choose ourselves in
opposition, how to reach out and link up with others in acts of repair. We move, then, beyond the facticity of the here and now toward a future our children will shape and inhabit. Our social imaginations are engaged—Can we envision a better social order? Can
we conceive a decent world, a place fit for all our children? Can we
dream a site of peace and justice?—and we begin to speak a nor-

mative language, an idiom of "should" and "ought." And then, if we are open enough and if the catalyst tugs hard enough, we can be stirred to action. I would, after all, have left the gruesome graffiti alone (as did 100 fellow travelers) had I not been prodded by a fresh-faced five-year-old whom I loved intensely and who, without any drama or theatrics, just assumed that his Poppy would do the right thing.

In *Racism Explained to my Daughter,* Tahar Ben Jelloun (1999) is drawn to the ravine of race, to the treacherous rift of racism, provoked into the breach now by an attractive and powerful agent: his own 10-year-old child. The spark is her searching curiosity as she marches in a demonstration hand in hand with Ben Jelloun through the streets of Paris. What is racism? she begins. What is race? Prejudice? Culture? A scapegoat? Genocide? Heredity? Genes? An ethnic group? One childish question leaps to another and another, and Ben Jelloun, to our collective benefit, keeps pace with her curiosity, pushes through the cotton wool of shackled consciousness, the pseudo-language of clichés and slogans, to offer simple responses we can wonder about and weigh. Take it as a guide and a conversation.

What is racism?

Each of us could, of course, write a book about race. Mine begins with my own childish question: "Why is Celeste brown?" Celeste cleaned our house and I had noticed something—a difference. "Shush," my mother scolded. "We don't talk that way." Growing up in an entirely constructed racialized surround, and one in which almost no one acknowledges its existence, means that we draw a commonsense experience of race into ourselves with our every breath, that we drink it in, beginning with our mother's milk. A society founded on the attempted genocide of the original people, built on the labor of African slaves, developed by Latino serfs and Asian indentured servants, made fabulously wealthy through conquest and exploitation, manipulation and mystification—a society like this one is a whole world built on race.

But race is unspeakable. "We don't talk that way." I'll say. We don't talk at all. I remember a moment of muteness when my three kids came home one day from junior high school with a story of a fistfight in the cafeteria. "Paul called Tony a 'polack,' and then Tony called Paul a 'nigger,'" Zayd reported, "and then they really got into it." After describing the fight and noting that both boys were suspended from school, they wanted to know, "Which is worse, 'polack' or 'nigger'?" What do you think? I countered, buying time once again. They had studied the Indian wars, the slave trade, and the Holocaust in Europe, and so we had a lengthy, engaged talk about the historical weight of words, the ways in which meaning can link to power and control, why calling a Jew a name in Germany, for example, might resonate with additional power. "Why do the black kids call each other 'nigger'?" one of them then asked, and this led to an involved discussion of both the cooptation and the sometimes internalization of hateful language. When I went to their school to urge a broader discussion so that all the kids could benefit from reflection on these difficult and complex issues, issues already abuzz in the informal curriculum of the cafeteria, I was told that talk would be troublesome. "We don't have a race problem here," the principal assured me. "And this might stir something up. Besides," she continued, playing to another presumptive set of fears, "math exams are coming up." A teachable moment discarded, lost. And in that screaming silence a lens of distorted images, fears, misunderstandings, and cool calculatedness slips neatly into place. We are, each of us, born into race and place, and all the early lessons are about knowing something of each. But we are rendered speechless.

Frederick Douglass, the great American abolitionist, found the roots of bigotry in the need to justify oppression:

> Pride and selfishness . . . never want for a theory to justify them—and when men oppress their fellow-men, the oppressor ever finds, in the character of the oppressed, a full justification for his oppression. Ignorance and depravity, and the inability to rise from degradation to civilization and respectability, are the most usual allegations against the oppressed. The evils most fostered by slavery and oppression are precisely those which slaveholders and oppressors would transfer from their system to the inherent character of their victims. Thus the very crimes of slavery become slavery's best defense. By making the enslaved a character fit only for slavery, they excuse themselves for refusing to make the slave a free man. A wholesale method of accomplishing this result is to overthrow the instinctive consciousness of the common brotherhood of man . . . (quoted in Gates, 1995, p. 94)

The elaborate edifice of racism as bigotry is built brick by brick upon the hard ground of race as a convenient invention for exploitation. Prejudice and the idea of inferiority based on race grow from and are fed by the desire to justify and perpetuate inequality, domination, control. And while discrimination and slavery go back to antiquity, chattel slavery based on race—that is, the enslavement of an entire people and their transformation into commodities without any family, property, or rights whatsoever, bound for life and for generations into the imaginable future, and simultaneously the invention of whiteness as an immutable marker of privilege—is the "peculiar institution" born in North America of the African slave trade. Racism as a primary social and cultural dividing line in America—developed from a greed for profit and achieved by deception and a monopoly of firearms, not by biological superiority, real or imagined—is the legacy of that institution.

That is some of what W. E. B. DuBois had in mind when he declared the problem of the 20th century "the problem of the color line." At the end of the century—a century marked by unparalleled degradation and violence against people because of color, ethnic background, and national origin, and by extraordinary efforts on the part of the downtrodden and disadvantaged of the earth to achieve and extend human dignity and freedom—and the start of the next, DuBois's words remain as lucid and significant as ever. "The problem of the color line" is more acute and entangled than ever, and requires an even more decisive response if DuBois's 20th-century problem is not to define and distort the 21st.

Racism is a many-horned devil, to be sure, a many-fisted monster, and a thoughtful response must necessarily be multidimensional. Racism is a disease, perhaps, a pathology. It is a sort of group madness, a kind of collective nervous breakdown. It is a myth, a lie (a white lie or a black lie), a distortion. It is an evil out there in the world with a strong life of its own. It is ignorance, blindness, witlessness. And it is more.

Racism can be found in our language: look at the dictionary, a seemingly authoritative source. Under "white" we find "free from spot or blemish," "free from moral impurity," "not intended to cause harm," "innocent," "marked by upright fairness"; and then phrases like "white knight," "white horse," and "white hope." "Black" doesn't fare so well: "dirty," "soiled," "thoroughly sinister or evil," "wicked," "sad, gloomy, or calamitous," "grim, distorted, or grotesque." Associated terms include "black art" (sorcery), "black and blue" (discolored from bruising), "blackball" (to exclude from membership), "blackmail" (to exhort by threats), "black market" (illicit trade), "black out" (to envelope in darkness), "black heart" (evil), "black day" (characterized by disaster), and on and on.

There it is, in our mother tongue, embedded in our language, the core of our ability to think and act with some semblance of harmony with others. A coward is "yellow," a victim of fraud is "gypped" or "Jewed." In a country brutally divided along racial lines, founded and sustained on a constructed hierarchy of color and calamitous class divisions, language itself is encoded with privilege, oppression, bias, bigotry, and power. Modern American English tells us who we are, where we have been, and where we might be going. Is it any wonder?

I taught for several years in a school where we worked diligently to create a liberating and empowering environment for young children, and we struggled constantly with our own language. The school was founded and directed by an extraordinary young woman renowned for her advocacy of multicultural and antibias perspectives; the multiracial community of parents and staff tended toward public activism for equity and social justice. We wanted, as well, to free ourselves from the artificial constraints of a racist and sexist society, and so it became natural and not jarring in our school to hear conversation laced with terms like "mail carrier," "police officer," "cowhand," and, my personal favorite, "waitron." Not only did "firefighter" replace "fireman" but our dramatic play area had a poster of a black firefighter in action, and our block area had a unique collection of little figures and wedgies including a White male nurse and a Black woman firefighter. "Firefighter, firefighter, firefighter."

Now, here's the problem: our school was across the street from a firehouse and the firehouse was staffed exclusively with White male firemen. We visited the firefighters, tried on their hats, rang the bell, and got to know a few of them. One day Caitlin, 5 years old, asked Jimmy, the fireman, when he expected there would be women in the station house, and he exploded in laughter: "Never, I hope. Women can't do this work. The neighborhood would burn down."

"That's not fair," Caitlin said later, and the class wrote letters of protest to the fire chief, the mayor, and the city council members pleading for justice, for the simple right of women to fight fires. Children are, of course, careful observers, diligent classifiers, and concrete learners, and reality is their most powerful teacher. Our nonsexist language and our nonracist materials were in combat with some hard facts, and changing language did not in itself change worlds. Our adult responsibility as far as their education is concerned includes the obligation to present the concrete situations they encounter as problems that challenge them and call for a response. The children of Little Rock or Soweto or our own little school show us the possibility of this type of education, and of children as actors in history as well, not merely observers or objects or victims.

Toni Morrison (1993) talks of the "evacuated language" of the powerful, of the "systematic looting of language" geared toward "menace and subjugation." "Oppressive language does more than represent violence," she writes, "it is violence; does more than represent the limits of knowledge; it limits knowledge." She argues for the rejection and exposure of "obscuring state language or the faux language of mindless media," "language designed for the estrangement of minorities, hiding its racist plunder in its literary cheek." She describes "sexist language, racist language, theistic language" as "typical of the policing languages of mastery" that "cannot, do not, permit new knowledge or encourage the mutual exchange of ideas" (p. 152).

Another child's question. Malik, our verbal, expressive three-year-old, attends the preschool where I teach. Part of the normal experience of youngsters in this community is active involvement in neighborhood events and activities. Soon we will attend a powwow at a nearby junior high school sponsored by the American Indian Movement.

When I tell the kids about the powwow they are excited and eager: there will be drums; there will be food to eat. But Malik, who typically loves ritual, oddly wants none of it. He whispers to me: "Will the Indians be wild, Poppy? Will they be scary?" No, I assure him. It will be engaging and interesting and we will have a good time. And we do. But Malik insists that I hold him for the first hour, just to be sure.

Where did he get the idea that the Indians would be wild or

scary? He's only three, after all, and we don't even own a television. He is named for Malcolm X (in Arabic, Malik el Shabazz) and his middle name is Cochise; he has pictures of Malcolm X and Cochise in his room, and has read many positive children's books about Native Americans. How did this stereotype get into his head?

Of course we have all seen the children's books filled with headdresses and hatchets; I remember an alphabet book with "I" for "Imitating Indians," and the accompanying illustration of animals whooping around and acting crazy—I think of a whole book modeled on this one entry: "J" for "Jumping Jews" wearing yarmulkes, or "N" for "Nice Negroes" eating watermelon. Disgusting. All Americans are part of the culture of disappearing Indians (ten little, nine little, eight little Indians—a particularly appalling popular poem filled with suggestions of genocide), wooden Indians, Indian givers, drunken Indians, cowboys and Indians, and all the rest. Most of us encounter *Little House on the Prairie* at some point, and Laura's shivery description of the wild, stinking, animal-like Indians of her imagination. We learn that Indians are somehow the enemy. We are set up, then, to accept the crass justifications for piracy and murder. Where do we get these ideas? They are, of course, knit deeply into the fabric of our culture: they are a toxic substance in the air we breathe; they come without asking and are available without effort. They are put in our heads early and often.

And so there is language, racist language and the language of racists, and still there is more. Language is not yet the bottom of the matter; it reflects, it mirrors, but it is neither fountainhead nor generator. We must push beyond language, go through the looking glass, as it were, in search of the source of such vivid and enduring speech.

Race bristles with significance, and yet when we speak of race we pull from a curious variety of meanings and a cacophonous base of knowledge. Race might refer, and often does, to a people or nation or tribe of the same stock and background—the German race, the Jewish race, the Japanese race, the French race, the American race. This has a preposterous edge, of course, for practically no one really believes any longer that those broad strokes of background are somehow immutable or implacable, that tribal stock is really static, or that national identity is stonelike. And yet not so long ago crime statistics in Chicago, for example, were broken down into categories that strike us today as odd: Irish, Italian, Jewish, Negro, White. They are now reported as Black, White, Hispanic, Asian. No less absurd. It all depends on the lens, on the angle of regard. It is hard to claim much in the way of progress here.

In truth, human beings permeate each other fairly freely, collide and burrow, pierce and enter one another in an enduring and dynamic dance of change and interchange. And it has always been so: we meet, we mate. And because we can, we do, and we are, then, of a single race: human. There are no other races, pure and simple.

Poets remind us of this ancient truth; here, for example, is Carl Sandburg:

> There is only one man in the world
> And his name is All Men.
> There is only one woman in the world
> And her name is All Women.
> There is only one child in the world
> And the child's name is All Children.
> There is only one Maker in the World
> And His Children cover the earth
> And they are named All God's Children. (Sandburg &
>   Steichen, 2002, p. 3)

And Langston Hughes:

> Consider me,
> A colored boy,
> Once sixteen,
> Once five, once three,
> Once nobody,
> Now me.
> Before me
> Papa, mama,
> Grandpa, grandma,
> So on back
> To original
> Pa . . .
> Consider me,

Descended also
From the
Mystery. (Hughes, 1994 quote in Jelloun, 1999, p. 156)

All the attempts through the centuries to divide human beings into the fiction of races—173 in one scientific rendering 200 years ago, 57 in another—would seem silly if they didn't represent such murderous and bloody projects. But they always do. The invention of whiteness as a permanent symbol of the fully human, the just-us, as a chit to be traded on in tough times, is the condition that creates the other, the stranger, the less-than-fully-human. David Malouf, in *Remembering Babylon* (1993), describes the unraveling of a settler community on the Queensland coast of Australia when a man stumbles from the outback who looks and talks like a native, but is, unmistakably, an Englishman who had been raised by Aboriginals from boyhood—without the neat division of "us" and "other," the town spins out of control. Wherever we find the marshaling of science to define visible human differences as races, we find conquest on the agenda and ruin at the horizon. The invention and glorification of race is ultimately a recipe for murder.

Every story of oppression begins with the cries and groans of unjustified suffering, undeserved harm, unnecessary pain—stories of human beings in chains or under the boot. It begins, say, with slavery, not an American invention, but rather a frightening commonplace in human experience. Americans, even today, like to point glibly to slavery's historic banality, its everydayness through the ages, as if that trumps the "peculiar institution" of slavery became in our own land, in the hands of our forefathers.

A word, especially one that points to something so large and so ghastly, can conceal as much as it reveals, can in spite of itself provide a protective gloss so that the unspeakable—in being spoken—is reduced and falsified. War, genocide, slavery—we search out the words to name the world, to understand, to grasp, perhaps to change what we find before us. But sometimes, through misuse or overuse, words become clichés, clichés then become slogans. The rough edges, the specificity, are sanded off and smoothed out; we utter the word without weeping. The imagination collapses and the mind closes down. Whatever horror the word pointed to in the first place becomes opaque; the word blinds us, begins to erase the world.

Just so, slavery. It is large, it is long. It is dreadful, of course; we can all agree there. But it has come to a condition of little depth, little detail.

So think of this particular young man, a young man with a specific human face, a mother and a father, a past and a future. He has a name that points to his ancestors, his father's father's name, and beckons toward a future of promise and redemption. He is in love, for the first time perhaps, and his new wife is pregnant with their first child, a sign of productivity and abundance, their hope for tomorrow. He works every day in the fields and the forests, minding crops and animals, gathering food, attending to the requirements of home and village. Almost every evening he smokes his pipe with the men before he rests.

And then in one blinding and violent moment his life is crushed. The sudden, searing struggle overwhelms him, cripples him, leaves him bloody and gasping. Whipped and chained and transported in the hold of a ship for 34 torturous days of puking and dying and starving and shitting on one another, he arrives in a strange and brutal place only half alive.

He endures, he survives. The pain is never entirely gone, but the mind shuts down and covers up, the raw and open wounds become scars. He lives for 42 more years, fathers two more children but knows neither one, dies without family or mourners, his remains placed in an unmarked slave yard near the fields.

How can we understand such a thing? Everything the young man had was taken, but more than this. Everything he was, everything he might have become was also stolen from him. What footprint did he leave in the sand? What meaning did he make? In slavery the attempt was made to transform him from a person of depth and dimension to a thing for the use of others. His humanity was reduced by the slave traders to a crude cash transaction, his hopes and dreams, his aspirations and capacities smashed on the ground. The rhythm of his life was ruined—it had no rhythm. What remained was the dumb repetition of labor without purpose, toil without hope.

This single act is a monstrous crime, of course. But rather than multiply this single crime by, say, 10 million lives, better to take it life by human life. Each story specific in its horror, each particular. And the telling of it makes the pain distinct, understandable in human terms.

And then there is the slave trader's side of the story, and the birth of institutional racism. I remember a film tracing a family's history back to Africa. Early in the story the captain of a slave ship, a man who considers himself a Christian and a liberal and finds, he claims, the transporting of slaves odious work, confronts his first mate, a crude, unpolished fellow who regularly rapes and abuses the human cargo, often throwing people who resist overboard, and taunts the captain for his squeamishness. The captain, all worry and hand-wringing, implores the brute to treat the slaves a bit better, insisting that they are also human beings and God's children. The first mate looks him squarely in the eye and responds with astounding lucidity: of course they're human beings, he says, and if we're to profit from this enterprise we'd best convince them and everyone else that they're dogs or mules, anything but human. You see, he points out, if they're fully human, there's absolutely no justification for our business. Only if they're inferior—in their own minds *and* in the minds of the exploited but relatively advantaged whites—will we stand to gain. We must, if we are to benefit, insist that they are "niggers." With that the captain retreats into his ineffectual anguish.

It begins with human beings mistreating others and then codifying and justifying that mistreatment in law and institutions. James Baldwin writes that "the brutality with which Negroes are treated in this country cannot be overstated, however unwilling white men may be to hear it." It begins in the real world, the blood and bone world, in the world of concrete material things.

In other words, while racism is indeed a bad idea, it is an idea brought forth and sustained by a rotten reality. The bad idea is neither its own source nor foundation. Rather it pivots on a base of injustice and operates simultaneously on many levels—the imposition of white supremacy is then rationalized by religion, culture, and myth, encoded in law, defended by force and violence. Fighting racism in the realm of language alone, or only in the world of ideas, without undermining the unjust structures that give birth to those ideas, is in the end a hopeless mission.

The endurance and strength of prejudiced ideas and values lie in their renewable life source: the edifice of inequality based on color, the structures of privilege and oppression linked to race and backed up by force. In Illinois, for example, we have created what amounts to two parallel school systems—one privileged, stable, well financed, and largely White, the other ineffective, chaotic, disadvantaged in countless ways, and largely African American, Latino, and poor. Racism is expressed through this duality, through inadequate resources for those most in need, through isolation, through unresponsiveness. When Governor James Thompson called Chicago schools "a black hole" while refusing to release more funds, he excited all the racist justifications that flow from and are fed by that unjust reality. Politicians continue to call Chicago schools "a rathole," "a sinkhole," and "a black hole"—rotten and bigoted language propping up a rotten and unequal structure.

Changing ideas and changing reality are distinct. The lifeblood of bigotry is the concrete situation it supports, but it is also true that when an idea is the accepted currency of a large enough number of people, it becomes a force of its own, with a real, palpable power over people's lives. For example, when virtually all of Europe believed the world was flat, that belief became itself a barrier beyond which exploration proved impossible. To break through the barrier required an assault on the old idea, but it was the actual going beyond the edge of the earth that proved decisive in discrediting and eventually destroying the incorrect idea.

The world of children is not neatly bounded from other worlds and larger realities, and the explorations of children are neither logical nor discrete. They explore the world, and their inquisitive wanderings are organic and unlimited. They know no bounds. One of the challenging and refreshing things about living with children is that they go on exploring, asking about whatever enters their fields without regard to what is controversial or what is in bad taste or what is off limits. Children's comments are often dazzling in their insightfulness, and their questions are often confounding in their illumination of human mystery. Why is Mom angry? Why didn't Dad come home last night? Why is he talking loud? Why is she in a wheelchair? Why is she asking for money? Is that fair?

Because racism is rooted in real (not imagined) oppression, and because that oppression is reflected in actual (not fantasy) inequality and injustice, it is not surprising that children discover the hard lessons about race and social value early. Kenneth and Mamie Clark

showed with poignant clarity that black preschool children understood not only that they were black, but that to be white was an
advantage in our society. By the age of four, children of all backgrounds tend to know who has cultural power and who has not,
who to befriend and who to fear, who to choose and who to refuse.

This confronts teachers and educators with an enormous teaching problem. Because education at its best creates public spaces for
people to come together with their own hopes and dreams and aspirations and experiences, education is essentially a process that opens
doors and opens minds—anything that constrains or limits or closes
is the enemy of education. Racism, sexism, and other forms of organized oppression are anti-education. For this reason alone teachers and educators must struggle for ways to understand, engage
with, and resist racism in their classrooms and in the larger world.

What is to be done?

I am drawn to another explanation offered to a child by another
prominent novelist and searing essayist. This one was in the form of
a "Letter to My Nephew on the One Hundredth Anniversary of the
Emancipation," and I, although eavesdropping, read and reread it,
captivated, in my youth. The author was the incomparable James
Baldwin, and the letter, "My Dungeon Shook," is the opening pages
of *The Fire Next Time* (1995). Baldwin wastes no time indicting the
United States: "This is the crime of which I accuse my country and
my countrymen, and for which neither I nor time nor history will
ever forgive them," he begins, "that they have destroyed and are destroying hundreds of thousands of lives and do not know it and do
not want to know it." Baldwin amasses a bill of particulars: "You
were born where you were born and faced the future that you faced
because you were black and for no other reason . . . you were born
into a society which spelled out with brutal clarity, and in as many
ways as possible, that you were a worthless human being." He tells
his nephew that "it was intended that you should perish in the
ghetto, perish by never being allowed to go beyond the white man's
definitions, by never being allowed to spell your proper name."
Baldwin argues that even though "the details and symbols of your
life have been deliberately constructed to make you believe what
white people say about you," that his nephew—along with other
Black people—must "remember that what they believe, as well as
what they do and cause you to endure, does not testify to your in-

feriority but to their inhumanity and fear." Too many White people, Baldwin believes, "are, in effect, still trapped in a history which they do not understand, and until they understand it, they cannot be released from it."

For Baldwin the remedy is painful and complex but available—Americans must look unblinkingly at their history, face our constructed reality, confront the tears of the wounded, the consequences of wickedness; we must harness ourselves, then, to a great collective effort toward justice. Baldwin finds hope in an image of "the relatively conscious whites and the relatively conscious blacks, who must, like lovers, insist on, or create, the consciousness of the others in order to end the racial nightmare, and achieve our country . . ." Action and commitment fueled by both rage and love, yes, but nothing until we summon the courage to look honestly at the world as it is: "It is not permissible that the authors of devastation should also be innocent. It is the innocence which constitutes the crime"; and "We, with love, shall force our brothers to see themselves as they are, to cease fleeing from reality and begin to change it."

We must, then, at some point come face to face with the world as it really is. We then see that race is simultaneously a vast fiction and our most enduring and profound truth. We fight to see through and beyond the fabrication of race, even as we must note without equivocation the powerful consequences of our humanly constituted, profoundly racialized world—*both*. We cannot pretend to be color-blind, but neither can we stumble in our attempts to transcend race.

The Nobel Laureate Wislawa Szymborska (1997) slices us humans up into various weird categories and then hits us with this deep, direct truth of our condition:

> Out of every hundred people,
> Those who always know better:
> Fifty-two.
> Unsure of every step:
> Almost all the rest.
> Ready to help,
> If it doesn't take long:
> Forty-nine.
> Always good,

Because they cannot be otherwise:
Four—well, maybe five . . .
Able to admire without envy:
Eighteen.
Led to error
By youth (which passes):
Sixty, plus or minus.
Those not to be messed with:
Four and forty . . .
Harmless alone,
Turning savage in crowds:
More than half, for sure.
Cruel
When forced by circumstances:
It's better not to know,
Not even approximately . . .
Those who are just:
Quite a few, thirty-five
But if it takes effort to understand:
Three.
Worthy of empathy
Ninety-nine.
Mortal:
One hundred out of one hundred—
A figure that has never varied yet. (p. 68)

Facing reality fully involves confronting our history, embracing
our past, including its deceptions and its discontents, its dishonesties
and its disasters. We see, then, that racism is not a little secondary
subplot in the American story but a central and permanent theme
coloring every other. We wake up, we open our eyes. We are not innocent, then, but neither are we paralyzed. As the legal scholar Der-
rick Bell (1992) writes

Perhaps those of us who can admit we are imprisoned by the history of
racial subordination in America can accept—as slaves had no choice
but to accept—our fate. Not that we legitimate the racism of the op-
pressor. On the contrary, we can only delegitimate it if we can accu-

rately pinpoint it. And racism lies at the center, not the periphery; in the permanent, not in the fleeting; in the real lives of black and white people, not in the sentimental caverns of the mind. (pp. 197–198)

Racism is a main channel in the American river, not a small trickle at the edge.

For Bell this recognition is not cause for despair, but rather for "engagement and commitment," and calls forth the same demand that Black people have faced since slavery: "making something out of nothing. Carving out a humanity for oneself with absolutely nothing to help—save imagination, will, and unbelievable strength and courage. Beating the odds while firmly believing in, *knowing* as only they could know, the fact that all those odds are stacked against them." Bell urges action to create meaning, to name oneself in opposition, to oppose the void. He counsels "the pragmatic recognition that racism is permanent" side by side with "the unalterable conviction that something must be done, that action must be taken."

We must stand up to oppose the evil of racism, an evil that is out there in the world as surely as it is in here, inside our minds and our hearts. But because it is out there, it is foolish to parse matters—I'm better than Mark Fuhrman, we're tempted to boast, I'm neither a Nazi nor a Klansman. The important thing is not to shade off into self-congratulation, but is rather to find the courage to be counted, to stir from indifference and inaction, to love the world enough to oppose the evil. Baldwin, again: "It is not necessary that people be wicked, but only that they be spineless" to bring us all to wrack and ruin. Amilcar Cabral, the African liberationist, noted, on the other hand, that you don't need to be a hero today to change the world; it is enough to be honest.

Those who embrace this colossal effort will be assisted if we will employ a two-eyed approach: one eye fixed firmly on the world as it is, the other looking toward a world that could be but is not yet— a future fit for all our children, a place of peace and justice. We can, with bell hooks, learn to create little sites of freedom, small locations of possibility: "to labor for freedom, to demand of ourselves and our comrades, an openness of mind and heart that allows us to face reality even as we collectively imagine ways to move beyond bound-

aries, to transgress. This is education as the practice of freedom"
(1994, p. 207). We can, with Tahar Ben Jelloun, respond to our children's questions directly and honestly. We can identify obstacles to
our collective well-being and link up with others in simple acts of
hope and love. We can, then, reclaim our humanity and, perhaps,
as Baldwin would have it, achieve our country.

PART III

TEACHER PROFESSIONALISM AND TEACHER EDUCATION

When I began teaching, it was common to refer to a specific, identifiable group of children as "culturally deprived," and universities offered practical courses on "Teaching the Culturally Deprived Child." Young teachers marched into their new classrooms primed and practically programmed to identify the "culturally deprived" kids in their midst. It wasn't all that tough: "culturally deprived" kids were poor, African American, Native American, or immigrants from Latin or Asian countries. Their presence leapt out.

Critics argued from the start that "culturally deprived" was freighted with more than a little negative judgment, more than a touch of stereotyping. After all, they explained, culture is not the authorized domain of some self-appointed elite, but is rather the vehicle through which all human beings make sense and make meaning in our vast variety and dazzling diversity. Spanish is a different language from English, to be sure, but not an inferior one; jazz is a particularly American classical music, not a broken idiom. We are an endlessly curious and inventive species, inexhaustible, everywhere capable of compassion and love and honor and beauty. "Culturally deprived" seemed to deny all this, and was, finally, understood to be a concept built on chauvinism and ignorance; it was defeated and fell into disuse. At that moment, the idea of multicultural education was born.

Of course, multicultural education can become its own cliché, sapped of energy and purpose, focused on the surface and the superficial. Many of us have seen classrooms with a "culture corner" of costume and artifact, always with an imagined and assumed standard that is American, White, middle class. In the Column A/Column B approach to multicultural education, children might count to 10 in Spanish or Swahili, don colorful shirts and dresses, dance the raspa or the hula. The representation of the friendly native—the exotic—plays against a foreground of normalcy—ourselves. Nothing much is challenged, nothing much has changed, and worse, students neither contribute much nor learn much through this approach.

This section is about the preparation of teachers and the profession itself. Teacher education is entirely implicated in the successes and failures of teachers and schools. Teacher education often perpetuates problems, but it might also become a site of resistance and resurrection.

CHAPTER 12

Rethinking the Profession of Teaching: A Progressive Option

Everyone, it seems, is concerned with professionalism in teaching, and yet what anyone means by professionalism remains elusive. Teacher professionalism is "a theme in search of specific policy initiatives and a social meaning appropriate to teaching circumstances" (Sykes, 1987). A focus on professionalism appears to make sense. First, those promoting teacher professionalism expect this focus to elevate the status of teachers. Second, they assume that a more solidly warranted profession will attract more able people to teaching and will bring greater rewards to teachers. Third, they believe professional status calls upon and justifies the research on teaching of recent decades. Finally, they hope that teacher professionalism will equip teachers to take control of the intellectual conduct of their work.

A focus on professionalism also raises difficult questions about the particular nature of teaching. Sykes (1987) discusses three critical ethical issues embedded in the ongoing movement toward teacher professionalism. First is the issue of caring. To many people caring and compassion are at the heart of the teaching enterprise, and teaching can only be understood in its focus on and interaction with actual children. Some critics are concerned that the move toward professionalism will be accompanied by a move away from this central aspect of teaching. Second is the issue of distancing. For those who think of teaching as unique among the professions precisely because it is a shared, inclusive, and democratic pursuit, there is concern that professionalism will remove teaching from the community that spawns and sustains it in favor of an obtrusive elitism. Third is the issue of equity. There is widespread concern that standard-setting will be used to discriminate against and drive out minority teachers and teacher candidates. Many critics argue that the move toward professionalism must be accompanied by a strong orientation toward justice if it is to avoid an objectively racist outcome.

*   *   *

In developing a sense of professionalism, it would seem important to determine the nature of teacher knowledge. Is it practical, multidimensional, and intersubjective, or is it primarily rational and technical? Teachers do indeed have a special knowledge, but is it principally an arcane, inaccessible knowledge? Is it knowledge limited to the conclusions of empirical studies? Is teacher knowledge mainly built up by teachers themselves, or is it primarily generated by outside experts and then transferred to practitioners?

Here is some of the knowledge effective teachers need:

- Knowledge of self
- Knowledge of human development
- Knowledge of the learning process
- Knowledge of historical, social, political, economic, and cultural contexts
- Knowledge of the disciplines
- Knowledge of the explicit and the hidden curriculum
- Knowledge of learning environments
- Knowledge of group process as well as individual behavior
- Knowledge of the interaction between affective and cognitive domains
- Knowledge of individual differences
- Knowledge of parents and communities
- Knowledge of children's meanings
- Knowledge of the complex interplay of the forces that motivate learning

Teaching is certainly much more than disconnected tasks, more than specific facts and findings generated by researchers, more than methods and behaviors. Teaching involves synthesizing of all kinds of knowledge, and its effective application in practice. Teaching involves creating opportunities for children to choose to learn, and it involves guiding children in their struggle to make sense, to become competent and powerful. Teaching occurs in contexts and involves making ethical judgments and decisions about what is of value and why. Conceiving of teaching in this way is not meant to discourage the quest for professionalism, only to resist a constrained, restricted model in favor of a vital and living one.

Many fine teachers find in their work the vital link between private and public worlds, between personal fulfillment and social responsibility. They bring a sense of commitment, of connectedness to other people and to shared traditions, and of collective goodwill. They also reject the sense of measured calculation that pervades so much of work today, embodying instead a sense of work closely tied to a sense of self, a view that work is not merely what one does, but who one is. And they accomplish all of this as an act of affirmation in a social and cultural surrounding that devalues their contribution and rewards them sparingly.

*   *   *

A sense of the teacher as decisionmaker and self-creator is a conception that opens to dizzying possibilities. It begins to reconceptualize research and social science generally as an exercise not in prescription but in public philosophy (Bellah et al., 1985). It moves in the direction of healing the split between research and teaching, between science and the humanities, and it begins that process by engaging in value-talk about what it is we want for our children, our work, and our world. Certainly it encourages teacher professionalism, not a distancing or passionless professionalism, not a "calculated and contingent" (Bellah et al., 1985, p. 69) professionalism, but one that insists at its heart on connectedness, collective goodwill, and social responsibility.

The traditional Aristotelian concept of friendship is a truer model of what we should seek in teacher professionalism. Friendship implies a concern for the person and for the community, a caring and compassionate attitude, a critical as well as careful and sympathetic regard. Friendship goes beyond a sense of deriving particular pleasure from another person and includes the sense of a mutual pursuit of the right and the good. Friendship, then, can be public as well as private, challenging as well as nurturing. In friendship there is space for the normative questions, for example, for the "ought" questions and the "should" questions. A model of friendship might capture more of what teachers actually do.

The current move toward a fuller and richer professionalism can be an important and healthy direction for teaching. It may help to affirm this most important and traditionally devalued enterprise. It may help empower teachers to take control of the intellectual content and conduct of their work. However, we must also beware of the unintended consequences such a direction could bring, such as diminishing the centrality of caring and compassion in teaching. If a concept of professionalism is built firmly on a base of respect for individuals and for community, of critique and compassionate regard, of connection and interaction, perhaps teaching may become the model of a new kind of professionalism for others to aspire to and emulate.

CHAPTER 13

Fact or Fancy:
The Quest for a Knowledge
Base in Teacher Education

In *Anthills of the Savannah*, Chinua Achebe's (1987) breathtaking novel about the struggle for human dignity and freedom in an African nation torn apart by poverty, ruthless ambition, betrayal, and a legacy of colonialism, he remarks on "the searing accuracy of the poet's eye," which is focused, he claims, "not on fancy but fact" (p. 194). He reminds us that the poet can tell us truths that are inaccessible in the bloodless language of objectivity. The poet can render facts in the language of fancy.

Equally interesting, of course, is the ability of the scientist to employ the colorful language of metaphor in order to further our collective understanding of complex phenomena. The physicist, for example, talks about "black holes in space" and describes high-energy particles as having "charm" and "strangeness" in an attempt to make the realm of science accessible. The recent breakthroughs in superconductivity were conceptualized and articulated in the imaginations of scientists, a creative process that transcended the hundreds of replications of identical experiments and relied in large part on a language of "what it is like." The scientist can stimulate and even expand the faculty of fancy.

Schoolteachers are the ultimate generalists; as such, they must have access to knowledge of a seemingly infinite range of evolving disciplines and literacies. Teachers are also decisionmakers, perpetually called upon to make choices about children, about learning, and about life in classrooms. Knowledge-of-teaching is constructed on an accumulation of practice, experience, and action. This knowledge—complex, hard-earned, and irreducible—is applied in unique ways to new situations. Thus, teachers need compassion and understanding as well as subject matter information; imagination and judgment as well as research-generated knowledge. Teachers need both fact and fancy.

There have been numerous attempts in recent years to create a workable text that would explicate an acceptable knowledge base for beginning teachers, a defensible "knowledge base" to directly inform both teaching and teacher education. According to an article in *Education Week,* one proposal would

> cover more than 20 specific topics, including knowledge of subject matter; theories and general principles of learning that cut across disciplines; research from instructional psychology, sociology, and anthropology giving insights into teaching; principles of classroom management and organization; knowledge about how children learn and develop; and information about the social and political contexts that influence teaching. (Olson, 1988, p. 7)

This brief and partial list is attractive to many people for a variety of reasons: it provides some organization in the untidy and messy business of teaching and teacher education; it promises to begin the consolidation of all the fragmented and detached bits and pieces of knowledge about teaching; it elevates the research on teaching efforts of the past two or three decades; and it forms the basis for the argument that teaching is a more fully developed and sophisticated profession.

But this list also illuminates the problems and difficulties we're likely to encounter in such a quest. For example, while the consolidation of a formal and universal knowledge base may clean up some of the messy business of teaching, it may at the same time unwittingly destroy the subtlety and nuance at the center of teaching practice. The spontaneous, person-specific, situationally particular nature of teaching might be sanded down and polished away in the desire for a smooth and flawless surface. While the authors of a knowledge base constructed on the findings of recent research on teaching might hope to create a more powerful practice, they may just as easily narrow our concept of teaching to those acts and behaviors that researchers find interesting, important, or researchable. What else might count as worthwhile inquiry? What is the relationship, for example, between formal research on teaching and the typically informal, anecdotal, imaginative everyday inquiry of teachers themselves?

An overriding problem is how to ensure that some universal knowledge base will be neither too broad nor too narrow. For example, one item on everyone's list would surely be classroom management and discipline—researchers and teacher educators agree that this is an important area of inquiry and practice, and teachers themselves describe classroom management as an essential part of their work. Classroom management is one of the most persistent perceived needs of preservice teachers; for many it is practically the *sine qua non* of teaching itself. Can there be any doubt about the necessity of including principles of classroom management in the developing knowledge base?

But once we move beyond the neutral, soothing term "classroom management," we're confronted with the problem of meaning. Classroom management is sometimes taught as a body of research-generated knowledge that can be applied fairly easily across situations. No consideration of culture, class, race, or ethnicity is needed in this approach—there is a "best practice" out there, suitable to all right-thinking people. This draws heavily on behaviorism and classroom effectiveness research and focuses on things like positive reinforcement, "wait-time," questioning strategies, and so on. Classroom management is viewed as a separate entity; accordingly, it is taught as a discrete and disconnected aspect of teaching.

Management issues, on the other hand, might be considered in the specific contexts of particular classrooms, in light of larger curriculum questions, and with particular children and a particular teacher in view. Classroom management could still be "taught," but it would be taught in response to situations experienced in classrooms. Management issues would emerge from natural contexts, and thus could be considered critically and concretely rather than strictly in terms of "law and order" in the classroom.

The problem of learning to live together might be considered a basic goal in some classrooms. Management, then, would not be so much an achievement once and for all, a prerequisite to real teaching, but rather the problem of learning to live together would become a curriculum that is forever being reshaped and retaught.

What does it mean to say that classroom management should

be a cornerstone of the knowledge base? Certainly classroom management rests on knowledge and thought as well as on values and judgment. Perhaps it should all be packed into our knowledge base. But if we include classroom effectiveness research, first-person accounts, conflicting and contradictory philosophies, revelation, intuition, and anecdotal knowledge emanating from situation-specific practice, are we not defeating the *raison d'être* for the knowledge base, namely, a more tidy, more research-generated view of teaching? Doesn't this leave us with a knowledge base that is unhelpful, vague and inexact, a knowledge base that is no base at all? And even if we could agree to narrow our perspective and focus exclusively on classroom effectiveness research, doesn't our account then become too narrow, too meager, too thin, too cramped, and thus not too helpful? The knowledge base appears to be either large, indistinct, and obscure, or small, scant—and still obscure.

The researcher who takes a laboratory approach to school reform and works from the assumption that school is a control experiment that can be analyzed and empirically tested is ignoring the contexts of schooling, the larger contexts of social class, race, gender, history, and economic condition, as well as the immediate hidden curriculum of obedience, hierarchies, compassion, and meaningless tasks. While it may be easier to graft particular reforms onto schools as they are, such as installing a five-second wait-timer in every classroom rather than rethinking and reorganizing what we are doing in teaching and schooling, we are then treating the problem cosmetically rather than systematically.

Robert Maynard Hutchins noted that contemporary life is so complex and subject to such rapid change that our thinking has not kept pace with our situations and our ideas have devolved into something more like slogans. Part of the allure of the knowledge base is its catchiness and its august connotation. But a knowledge base also implies something sanctioned by positivistic science; indeed, those who most vigorously promote the knowledge base image refer to a dramatic explosion of research on teaching that justifies the construction of a knowledge base. In actuality, the relationship between teaching and research is indirect, partial, and fragmentary. In focusing on the importance of empirical research, we risk losing sight not only of the personal dimension of teaching, but also of the ethical, aesthetic, moral, and political dimensions as well.

Those who have adopted the language of a knowledge base have done so in part to elevate the profession of teaching. Ironically, an unexpected consequence of this language could be the increasing perception of teaching as a relatively flat and straightforward occupation, a routine job without texture, depth, artistry, or uniqueness. Because the practice of teaching is so much more complex, deliberate, enigmatic, and personal than empirical research can adequately articulate, we may in fact do teaching a disservice when we narrow our discussion to a positivistic metaphor. Why not invent a new language of teaching and research that is rich with possibility and power, a language that opens up discussion, question, and critique, that conveys ambiguity, irony, mystery, tension, and growth? In this way we might resist a language that cuts off argument and closes conversations. What we would seek, then, is an infinitely layered and richly textured dialogue; what we would oppose is the last word.

Chinua Achebe (1987) offered this admonition concerning fact and fancy:

> Those who mismanage our affairs would silence our criticism by pretending they have facts not available to the rest of us. And I know it is fatal to engage them on their own ground. Our best weapon against them is not to marshal facts, of which they are truly managers, but passion. Passion is our hope and strength, a very present help in trouble. (p. 385)

What constitutes the knowledge base of teaching and teacher education? The answer is hard to pin down. Some will argue that more empirical research is the remedy. But that argument begs the question, for the project of knowledge base definition is in fact many projects. Indeed, it is not a project that will ever be completed, given that knowledge is in a constant state of flux, constructed by people in time and place and surrounding.

How do we begin to reform teacher education? As in everyday teaching situations, we want to begin with students' lives, their needs, their individual and shared experiences. We know that students worry about a potentially hostile job market and about their academic success. We recognize the persistence of students' perceived needs for answers, for methods, for practical work, for classroom strategies, for "what works." We realize that much of what we consider valuable for teachers to know and experience, an engagement with the arts and imagination, for example, or concrete practice with cooperative teaching, is considered unnecessary and perhaps frivolous by many students.

In starting with students' lives, needs, and experiences, however, we also indicate a place where they might begin when they are teachers. But it is only the starting point; it is not where we stay: We consider teaching a dialogue of push and pull, back and forth, action and reaction. School typically devalues what children know and values what they don't. We begin by valuing what is known and then directing students' attention to discovery as a method of seeking the unknown.

When we think of all that a teacher needs to know, it is not surprising that the construction of a knowledge base eludes us. Certainly, teachers need a broad and general knowledge of the various disciplines that human beings use to make sense of themselves and their worlds. They must have access to the various subject matter literacies as well as the various ways of looking at teaching and learning, children and growth, thought and behavior, existence and condition. Teachers need to have access to these literacies not as canonical texts, but as living preceptors to action, commitment, construction, conflict, dialogue, and reconstruction. In this way, teachers can open themselves and those they teach to the possibility of active engagement with reality, of meaningful growth and essential change.

As teacher educators we choose to direct the attention of our students to areas often disregarded or dismissed and yet essential if teachers are not to be dehumanized and are to remain open to growth and choice. We are concerned that the construction of a knowledge base will not contribute productively to this effort. Knowing oneself, knowing how to think, how to imagine, and how to make critical judgments, can help teachers defend themselves against the often dreadful and adverse conditions of their teaching. We must examine the knowledge base with "the searing accuracy of the poet's eye." If we imbue the "bloodless language" of fact with the colorful imagery of fancy, perhaps we can contribute to a more authentic language of teaching.

CHAPTER 14

The "Long Trip": An Exploration of Progressive Public Schools

In 1935 Lucy Sprague Mitchell organized a "long trip" to Appalachia for members of the Cooperative School for Student Teachers (CSST), later the Bank Street College of Education. Accustomed to intense observations and explorations of their own communities in order to experience the excitement of learning as children might, now the entire student body and staff would engage in a sustained exploration of a different culture and a distant region. Mrs. Mitchell thought that things like mountain culture, the mining economy, and rural poverty would be forever foreign and abstract to these New York City students unless they were given opportunities to discover and interact with them directly. And so the entire school piled onto a bus and traveled to West Virginia, where they attended union meetings, toured the mines, and visited the miners' homes and their children's schools. On their way back to New York they stopped in Washington, D.C., where they sat in on committee meetings and toured government agencies, hoping to deepen their understanding of what they had seen and experienced in Appalachia.

The long trip was soon an important part of the curriculum and, for several years, an annual event at Bank Street College, for it contained in concentrated form many of the elements central to the "Bank Street approach" to teacher education. These elements included the notion of learning through discovery, direct experiences and contact with primary sources, a focus on multicultural and global perspectives in education, and a commitment to communities beyond the school. Perhaps most important to the Bank Street approach was the development of an interactive teacher, a whole person capable of ongoing growth, experimentation, creativity, and active learning. To accomplish this, Bank Street emphasized neither methods nor discrete subject matter disciplines. Rather, Bank Street faculty created opportunities for students to learn about the world in an invested, wholehearted, and integrated manner. While they did not glorify the results of research carried out at a distance by "expert" social scientists, they did encourage students to use the scientific method in their own work, that is, to maintain an experimental open-mindedness, to research their own children and their own situations, to think of conclusions as contingent and temporary, to question the old in light of further evidence, and to base action on alert observations and detailed recordings of the actual world. The long trip was a vivid example of the Bank Street approach in action.

I teach teachers at the University of Illinois at Chicago (UIC), and the long trip came to mind because of a student-initiated field trip to conduct a firsthand study of child-centered public schools. I came to UIC after many years in New York City, where my children attended day care and elementary schools, and where I worked in early childhood education and studied at the Bank Street College of Education.

While Chicago felt like home, New York City was in some ways still my point of reference in terms of education and schools. In the classes I taught I often drew upon experiences and examples from New York public schools. In my meetings with neighborhood groups, political and business people, individual teachers, and teachers' organizations in Chicago, I referred to the parallels—the perils as well as the possibilities—with the schools I had known in New York. While I was finding my way in Chicago, I still had, for better or worse, a New York state of mind.

So in a sense it was no surprise when a student came into my office on a cold day in March and asked, "Would you be willing to take a group on a field trip to visit innovative public schools in New York City?" She went on to explain that she and some friends had been talking about what they wanted to accomplish in their first year of teaching in Chicago public schools. They were active, outstanding students in one of my classes, and they had all been taken with the notion that learning is a process of active discovery, that it depends on concrete experiences and contact with primary sources if it is to be lasting and meaningful and, most important, if it is to lead to further growth and learning.

In that class we watched films, read articles, and talked about schools where hands-on learning with children is the norm and not the exception. We also experimented with discovery learning at our own, adult level. I felt then, as I do now, that it would be virtually impossible to teach in this way if you had never experienced the power of this approach as a learner. One assignment, for example, asked each student to develop an authentic question about the world, a question of some urgency or personal meaning, and then to go out and find the answer to that question by getting close to it, by touching it, and to document the whole process in a variety of ways. Later, students would use their question and the process they pursued as a model to develop curriculum with youngsters.

While all students—schooled as most of us are in passivity and conformity—found it a painful process to think of a question ("I don't know what you want us to do." "Would 'the jury system' be an okay question?" "I'm not interested in anything."), some students eventually asked burning questions and were able to pursue sustained inquires with astonishing results. One student, for example, whose sister was anorexic investigated anorexia and became involved in an innovative support project for families. Another asked what life was like for the children of alcoholics, and discovered what she always suspected but denied: that her own mild-mannered, middle-class father was a quiet alcoholic. A hearing-impaired student looked into the reactions of a middle-class, residential neighborhood when a live-in facility for mildly disabled adults was established.

I particularly remember one student named Elaine. Her first attempts at an authentic question had been, "What is the meaning of the Constitution?" and "How are race relations going in Chicago?" Finally she asked, "Where does the woman in the green shoes who I see every day outside Sam Marcy's Restaurant sleep at night?" This question led her beyond a statistical and distanced view of homelessness and into a consciousness-expanding personal journey with Irene, the woman with the green shoes.

She discovered a thriving shantytown within half a mile of the university, a place of community and collectivity as well as of pain and poverty. She traveled to soup kitchens and church basements, scrounged trash outside hotels, panhandled at the train station. She uncovered personal histories: Irene's story of the closing of a mental hospital where she was being treated for schizophrenia; John's story of losing his job as a security guard when his firm lost a contract at the airport; Sharon's story of an abusive husband and an ongoing struggle with alcohol.

Elaine took pictures and recorded and transcribed interviews. She later developed a dazzling curriculum project filled with energy, experimentation, creativity, and open-endedness. It included an oral history component, a service project at a food pantry, an investigation of government policies and their impact on homeless people, and a weekend with the Mad Housers of Chicago, a group of housing activists who construct simple and livable (but not licensable) structures for the homeless.

The student who proposed the New York trip had this experience in mind when she said, "My question is, 'How do these more open classrooms actually work?'" She went on to argue that she would be better prepared to try some innovations in her own work the following year if she had direct experiences with actual classrooms where this approach is practiced. I was of course hooked, for here was an authentic student-initiated question to be investigated. Within days the ball was rolling toward a long trip to Central Park East School (CPE) in Spanish Harlem.

Central Park East is a public school founded by Deborah Meier and five other teachers in 1974. CPE is by design a small school, occupying one wing of a giant education complex that sprawls across a city block. The school's founders argued that it made sound pedagogical sense for a school to be small enough so that every member— every teacher, parent, and student—could understand and make sense of the whole. A small school would allow every child the opportunity to develop a sense of community and to be known by the adults in his or her life; it would allow parents more than formal access; and it would allow teachers the possibility of genuine sharing and a powerful voice in decisionmaking. They came up with a revolutionary idea: a school building is not identical to a school. This began a process of creating minischools based on different assumptions and philosophies that would share factorylike spaces with other schools, a concept that spread to many parts of the New York City system. When student demand for admission to CPE outstripped its ability to respond, Meier and her colleagues founded Central Park East II in 1979, and then River East in 1982. In 1986 they opened a secondary school, Central Park East Secondary School. The Central Park East schools now offer an alternative choice for the parents and children of Spanish Harlem from prekindergarten through high school.

When I called Central Park East, the staff had just created the Center for Collaborative Education in the Public Schools, a network of New York schools working around similar objectives. The Center was trying to find new ways to respond to the growing interest in these schools, as well as ways to communicate their successes more broadly by, for example, offering concrete assistance to teachers outside the network schools who are struggling to change their own practices and implement similar goals. People at the Center were enthusiastic about hosting a group of new Chicago teachers interested in their schools, and we speculated about the possibility of future exchanges, CPE teachers visiting our classrooms in the fall, for example, and helping people get started. We agreed that for this trip the Center would find classrooms where each person could assist and observe for a week. At this point we didn't know whether 2 or 20 students would respond to the invitation, but the Center was willing to accommodate whoever came along.

I sent a letter to all the students I had taught that year inviting them to participate. I would be responsible for working with the Center to set up a schedule of classroom visits and meetings with educators, and further, I would find housing with teachers I knew in the area. Students would be responsible for transportation and living costs for a week. In June six students and I ventured to New York for a week of immersion in a different kind of schooling.

Our base was CPE-I, where we observed and worked in classrooms for a week. This is some of what we saw and experienced: Learning is active. The classrooms at CPE are alive with animals, plants, projects, color, and motion. There are no neat rows of desks, no passively quiet youngsters. Bruce's sixth-grade classroom, for example, looks like a combination biology lab, art center, museum, and living room. Big couches and carpet fragments define an area where children read and write research reports. Computers take up one corner, while board games and math materials dominate another. Child-made tiles recently fired in the kiln are being laid out in a collage on one table. The sink, refrigerator, and microwave oven help define the kitchen area, which is the focus of almost constant activity. Plants, fish, turtles, and snakes share the space. The children move about the room working on projects, attending to housekeeping chores, checking in with one another. Bruce moves around the room, too, guiding, helping, nudging, criticizing, supporting, and giving direction to the whole. Later, when we ask Bruce about specific children and incidents, he reveals an astonishing knowledge of each child and a kind of evolving teaching strategy for each moment. He is not dominating the space, but he is clearly providing leadership to each child and to the whole group. Bruce is the key to classroom life—he sets up the environment and the routine, he develops the expectations and the pace—but for him it is the activity of the children that counts as learning.

Jarring for new visitors is the level of noise and activity. Accustomed to classrooms of passive and quiet youngsters, or at least to classrooms where the struggle to keep order is paramount and where the mark of teacher success is the effective management of noise and movement, it is initially unsettling to be in a setting where real learning is assumed to require active and interactive youngsters. Here children move around a lot and talk with one another at will. And why not? Is every 10-year-old, say, ready to learn the same thing at the same moment? Is quietly receiving bits and pieces of information from a teacher an effective way to learn? At CPE, learning is assumed to require interest, investment, and wholeheartedness. There are no superficial "readiness" techniques in use. Rather, teachers work ceaselessly to understand real kids, to adjust their teaching in order to engage the passions and imaginations of youngsters, and to create projects and activities that respond to the needs and intentions of specific children.

Learning is integrated. The children's projects at CPE involve a natural synthesis of what we traditionally think of as separate subject matter disciplines: language arts, math and science, social studies, art. In Donnie's second-grade classroom, for example, the children have been caring for a chicken all year. The room is resplendent with drawings and stories of chickens. There is an entire shelf of chicken-related books: some are science books about the life cycle of chickens, some fiction, in which chickens are central or peripheral characters. The week before our arrival, the chicken had hatched a brood of chicks, and there is now great activity following the progress of the babies, charting their growth, measuring and tending, and deciding who will take one home for the summer.

The sixth graders, meanwhile, are getting ready to graduate. Each student is constructing a chair for the graduation ceremony. This involves reading and research, thought and creativity, math and science, and a lot of hard work. At the end of one corridor on the second floor, the pile of chairs is reaching completion: one looks like a throne for a queen, another that is an old-fashioned school desk, one that has a curving rainbow for a back.

Bruce's class is hosting a busload of children from Long Island on a tour of Spanish Harlem. These youngsters corresponded all year with the children in Bruce's class. Bruce's group raised money through bake sales and raffles and car washes in order to rent a bus to visit their pen pals. Now the children from Long Island are visiting here. This project involved reading and writing, bookkeeping and budgeting, studying a different culture and region as well as communicating about one's own, and sustaining a complex year-long activity in an engaging, imaginative way.

In each of these projects children are allowed to pursue learning linked to matters of importance to them. The graduation chairs for most of the sixth graders represent real work, work of interest, meaning, and value. Real work requires real effort and provides genuine payoff. The teachers at CPE believe that when children are engaged in work that has value to them, no one fails.

The classroom is a community. Classrooms are diverse, and there is an obvious celebration of diversity. Black, White, Hispanic, Asian, and Native American children share, grow, and interact together. Individualized learning allows for a wide range of abilities and interests to be met within each classroom, and so there is no takeout time for slow readers, no obviously identified "learning-disabled" children.

Because the classroom is a community, teaching and learning are more than cognitive activities. Children are conceived as whole people with emotions, hopes, dreams, intentions, cultures, bodies, spirits, and intellects, and so learning is not thought of as narrow or isolated. Teachers believe that feeling good about oneself, one's culture, and one's body is also a necessary part of learning.

Living in a community provides concrete practice for life in a democracy. At CPE teachers argue that empowerment is not something that can be magically bestowed on a person upon high school graduation. The ability to make decisions, to live with consequences, to participate in the group, is something to be practiced right from the start. The youngest children make a range of choices, from which materials and projects to work with, to when to eat and go to the toilet. In Bruce's class more complex questions take up the meeting time. How should we spend the surplus money? What should we do about the two children who were disruptive during the lunch sale?

The community is part of the classroom. Parents are welcome, and participate freely in a variety of classroom and school activities. Teachers and children also freely use the city: Yvone's kindergarten uses the skating rink in Central Park every Friday afternoon during the winter; Bruce's group walks to museums on Fifth Avenue every week; one class made several visits this year to La Marqueta, the sprawling outdoor marketplace, and re-created it in blocks back at school. The city and the neighborhood become for these teachers a resource rather than a deficit.

In many ways the high point of our New York trip was a meeting we attended one evening between parents and teachers who eventually started a public school similar to CPE in the fall called the Bronx New School. This school is the result of years of effort by parents to create a progressive alternative in their district. At the meeting the teacher-director talked about the importance of allowing children's interests to carry them from the superficial to the deep, and about the importance of weaving traditional disciplines into a comprehensive whole. She talked about teachers empowering youngsters to take control of their lives and their own learning, and about learning by doing, by exploring, and by experimenting rather than by being told. She talked about the parks, shopping districts, and public library as resources they would use in their teaching.

Finally, parents and teachers spent hours exploring the perennial questions: What if a child won't learn? What about discipline? How will we prepare kids for the realities of the world? The meeting was full of dreams and hope and, most important, a willingness to work hard together for the children.

For five days we were immersed in a different kind of schooling, which became for the moment our reference point and the common sense. Wherever we went, those of us from UIC saw classrooms organized as laboratories for learning rather than mini–lecture halls, teachers who shared with one another rather than shutting their doors against the world, children as active and noisy rather than passive and inert. We came to expect snakes and rabbits and gerbils and chickens. And we came to expect a sense of community and compassion among the people with whom we spoke.

These schools are of course not new. They share elements with other "effective schools"—strong leadership, for example, and high expectations for students—but they go beyond these traditional schools in their focus on how children learn and in their commitment to a child-centered approach. Many of the best private schools in the country are organized along these lines, and many of the best teachers practice these principles in their own classrooms. What is new here is the development and expansion of this kind of education in poor urban public schools at a time when the mood in the country is toward a narrow and constrained sense of learning linked to a punitive, sometimes brutal system of accountability. This is cause for celebration.

During World War II the long trip at Bank Street came to an end. Lucy Mitchell had become too old to continue, and there were other projects and other demands on staff. Our own long trip was only a shadow of those other journeys, but for us it was an exciting time of discovery, integration, and experimentation. We were energized by the examples of people struggling to create good schools for city children, and humbled by the enormity of that task. We returned to Chicago feeling that we had built a small community of our own, a community committed to a project of ongoing growth, experimentation, and improvement in our own teaching.

CHAPTER 15

Headaches: On Teaching and Teacher Education

One of the characters in Chinua Achebe's (1987) A*nthills of the Savannah* explains the correct role for the writer: the writer, he argues, is not properly one who apologizes for the regime or soothes society's conscience or offers glib answers to complex questions; many people, perhaps most people, will press for rules and directions and solutions, but the writer must resist, in order to remain true to his or her calling. The writer, Achebe claims, must be a questioner, a witness, and a critic. The writer does not prescribe aspirin, but rather gives headaches.

This description neatly sums up one view of the responsibility of a teacher, one in which the teacher in this subverts what others take for granted, problematizes matters, and questions received reality. The teacher, like the writer, can be a philosopher, a scientist, an artist, a citizen, and even an activist, but only if she or he stays alive to possibilities, attuned to what has yet to be achieved in terms of freedom, justice, enlightenment, and beauty. One goes to this kind of teacher for questions, not answers, for possibilities, not prescriptions, because this teacher is assumed to be both seeker and guide, disciple and mentor. In a sense this teacher, like Achebe's writer, chooses a path that gives a self-inflicted headache on the way to dispensing headaches more broadly.

This kind of teacher could never be a clerk or a bureaucrat, mindlessly following directives or filling prescriptions according to a standardized manual. This teacher recognizes children are whole people with bodies, minds, emotions, intentions, hopes, dreams, cultures, and souls, and she works to discover the unique needs and tasks of each child and each situation. This teacher builds a laboratory for learning in the classroom, a place that supports and challenges the activities and efforts of a wide range of learners, and creates a place that builds on the knowledge children bring and extends to deeper and wider ways of knowing. The intellectual and practical challenge for this teacher is to create an authentic meeting with each child in a complex and changing environment, to know when to support and when to challenge, to figure out how to deepen learning and enlarge understanding. Such a teacher, then, must be a person of compassion and decision. Her classroom could never be "teacherproof," for she stands with the children at the heart of the action, and judgment—intellectual and ethical—is fundamental to everything that occurs.

Preparing teachers of judgment and thought, of care and compassion, has long been a concern of those who educate teachers, and yet it has been ignored or supplanted by issues of more apparent urgency in many colleges and universities. In some institutions, teacher education has been conceived as a fairly simple, straightforward, connect-the-dots kind of affair, heavy on methods courses and acceding to the everyday demands of the practical life of teaching, while offering little in terms of foundations, history, or philosophy. In other places, teacher education has been largely ignored in favor of a powerful research agenda, where teaching is conceived as the relatively simple application of research findings. In most places, theory and practice are structurally fractured into a sequence of courses that starts with history, touches on psychology, obsesses on methods, and then assumes that the split will somehow be healed through student teaching.

This season of reform and backlash may reawaken a concern for teaching as an intellectual and ethical enterprise, and for teacher education as essentially the preparation of thoughtful and caring artist/professionals. Our impulse to push for reform may move us "beyond where [the debate about reforming teacher education] customarily stops—on issues of the liberal arts versus education courses, graduate versus undergraduate preparation, selecting brighter people, testing" and carry us into "the central teacher education reform agenda involving curricular, instructional, organizational, and equity issues" (Goodlad, 1988, p. 80).

This "central teacher education reform agenda" necessarily involves a focus on basic, foundational questions like these:

- What is schooling for?
- What constitutes outstanding teaching?
- What kind of person do we want to become a teacher?
- How does one become an excellent teacher?
- What contexts make possible or constrain effective teaching and learning?
- What philosophy of education informs and is embedded in specific practice?
- How do children learn?
- What knowledge and experiences are of most value?

A focus on these kinds of questions offers particular challenges. One challenge is to move beyond the commonplace of schooling and teaching (and even of reform) in order to rethink teaching and teacher education fundamentally. It is to give ourselves a headache in the interest of concrete and authentic improvement.

The philosopher of science Thomas Kuhn (1970) reveals a perennial paradox in science: the quest for truth in science is almost everywhere subverted by the scientific disciplines themselves by their accepted laws and conventional rules, their authoritative texts and customary practices. Kuhn argues that scientific orthodoxy, which leads to replicating the known and proving the provable, is in conflict with the scientific mission of asking obscure, even unanswerable, questions. In other words, swimming in the sea of any discipline, essential somehow if one is to communicate with and use the tools of a given scientific community, weakens one's originality, creativity, and potential contribution to science.

Revolutions in science, those breakthroughs that move all human knowledge and thinking forward, occur when the steady accretion of bits of knowledge is seen as inadequate and there is, for some at least, a desire to go beyond. Imagination and courage are summoned, and inevitably the fundamental questions are asked again. In education, engaging the fundamental questions may lead us to look at old truths in original ways, and thereby contribute to our own revolution in thinking.

A serious and sustained argument with these kinds of questions can lead beyond many of the assumptions of teaching and teacher education, beyond a reliance on psychology and social science, for example, as foundational in teaching. It can open us to knowledge about and practice in areas typically ignored in teacher education, which in turn can lead to surprises about what is overlooked and reduced when teaching is conceived as either an applied science or a series of methods. Several devalued, largely missing areas are worth reconsidering as we reconstruct curriculum for teacher education.

AUTOBIOGRAPHY

Because no teacher can or should entirely escape or transcend subjectivity, teachers, whatever else they teach, teach themselves. Teaching involves a meeting of subjects, a meeting of different intentions, agendas, maps, dreams, desires, hopes, fears, loves, and pains—and in that meeting teachers necessarily model what they themselves value. Experienced, thoughtful teachers tend to be aware of this and work to make explicit, at least to themselves, their values, priorities, and stories, because they know that these things will impact their teaching practice. Being aware of oneself as the instrument of one's teaching, aware of the story that makes one's life sensible, allows for greater change and growth as well as greater intentionality in teaching choices.

Working on autobiographical texts can be a way of making values, beliefs, and choices accessible to teachers and prospective teachers alike. These texts—complex, idiosyncratic, alive, and changing— provide the kind of detail from which one can interpret practice. Autobiography is a way to engage the intricate interaction of inner and outer worlds, of feeling, thought, experience, belief, and action. Autobiography then can be a tool for improving practice.

Lortie (1975) advocated using student autobiographies as well as literature and biography in teacher education as a way "to increase the person's awareness of his (or her) beliefs and preferences about teaching and to have him (or her) expose them to personal examination" (p. 231). This, he believed, would allow the teacher to "become truly selective and work out a synthesis of past and current practices in terms of his (or her) own values and understandings" (p. 231).

Lortie compares teaching (unfavorably) to other human services professions:

> Social workers, clinical psychologists, and psychotherapists are routinely educated to consider their own personalities and to take them into account in their work with people. Their stance is supposed to be analytic and open; one concedes and works with one's own limitations—it is hoped—in a context of self-acceptance. The tone of teacher interviews and their rhetoric reveals no such orientation; I would characterize it as moralistic rather than analytic and self-accusing rather than self-accepting. (p. 159)

Madeleine Grumet (1978) notes that "autobiography, like teaching, combines two perspectives, one that is a distanced view—rational, reflective, analytic, and one that is close to its subject matter—immediate, filled with energy and intention" (p. 212). For Grumet, autobiography establishes the legitimacy of the teachers' own questions, their "stories, reminiscences of grade school, travel, family relationships, tales of humiliation, triumph, confusion, revelation" (p. 209). Autobiography also establishes a public record, the possibility for dialogue within collectivity.

Peter Abbs (1974) argues for a view of education that connects thought with feelings and intentions. Abbs denounces teacher training as methods courses preoccupied with facts and techniques, and advocates instead a deeper model of education that could somehow relate being and knowing, existence and education. For this, Abbs sees a central role for autobiography:

> How better to explore the infinite web of connections which draws self and world together in one evolving gestalt than through the act of autobiography in which the student will recreate his past and trace the growth of his experience through lived time and felt relationship? What better way to assert the nature of true knowledge than to set the student plowing the field of his own experience? (p. 6)

Personal knowledge is not easily described or examined, and yet teaching practice is constructed precisely on personal knowledge. Autobiography is a potentially useful process for helping teachers connect with personal knowledge, making it accessible in the search for understanding and meaning in their practical work.

INQUIRY

If teaching is conceived as a complex and kaleidoscopic endeavor, one that requires continuous awareness, reevaluation, and adjustment on many levels simultaneously, then knowing how to inquire into unique situations is indispensable. If teaching is like a craft in which there are levels of mastery and competence, but no last word or final point beyond which one cannot grow, then there is always surprise, always novelty, always something more to learn. Sustained inquiry, formal and informal, then, is an important part of learning about teaching, and must become a central area of concern in teacher education.

Inquiry develops the habit of learning. Duckworth (1987) describes in delightful detail situations in which children's ideas are accepted, their activity, open experimentation, and discovery encouraged. In these situations, Duckworth says, children set tasks for themselves and find surprising and important answers to their own questions. "The having of wonderful ideas," she claims, is "the essence of intellectual development" (p. 1).

To a young child, for example, the astonishing discovery at the easel that blue and red make purple is "the having of a wonderful idea." Instructing children in primary and secondary colors is an anemic alternative—it denies children the opportunity to have their own wonderful ideas. Similarly, when we process packaged knowledge and use perceptible methods, when we offer bits and pieces of molecular knowledge, when we value skills and facts over understanding or a search for meaning and perspective, we deny teacher education students their own discoveries.

Maxine Greene (1978) writes about the ways awareness, interest, and inquiry are linked to the possibility of an ethical life:

> We are all familiar with a number of individuals who live their lives immersed, as it were, in daily life, in the mechanical round of habitual activities. We are all aware of how few people ask themselves what

they have done with their own lives, whether or not they have used their freedom or simply acceded to the imposition of patterned behavior and the assignment of roles. Most people, in fact, are likely to go on in that fashion, unless (or until) "one day the 'why' arises," as Albert Camus put it, "and everything begins in that weariness tinged with amazement." Camus had wide-awakeness in mind as well, because the weariness of which he spoke comes "at the end of the acts of a mechanical life, but at the same time it inaugurates the impulse of consciousness." (pp. 42–43)

Later Greene adds that "lacking wide-awakeness . . . individuals are likely to drift, to act on impulses of expediency," and that they will be "unlikely to identify situations as moral ones or to set themselves to assessing their demands" (p. 43). One way to oppose indifference, passivity, amorality, and conventional consumerism in teachers is to encourage them to be creators of their own teaching, to promote a notion of teachers as actors and investigators in their own worlds, to offer students of teaching knowledge about and practice with inquiry.

A concern with inquiry indicates a view that teaching is problematic and not settled. That is, because no two teaching situations are ever quite identical, successful teaching cannot be completely prescribed, but must be discovered again and again as the result of a teacher's ability to extract knowledge from unique and messy situations, and then to make specific choices and judgments. Teachers need to understand as much as possible about themselves, the children they teach, and the social and historical contexts that enable and constrain their teaching.

Even within the walls of a classroom, teaching is uncertain. Outstanding teachers probe their classroom situations, interrogate their practice, and continually search for other, better ways. It is insufficient to begin teaching as if school reality is given, immutable, or the center of all action and growth, with children's lives, experiences, and contexts one-dimensional, irrelevant, or deficient. Nor is it acceptable to gear teaching toward definitive, sometimes punitive judgments. Inquiring teachers tend to develop formative evaluations of children, always in the service of framing new teaching problems, deciding what is to be done, and directing action to be tried and assessed again.

A concern with inquiry also points teachers to an important fact about learning: learning requires the interest and activity of the learner. Teachers create environments and opportunities for learning, but it is the curiosity, the motivation, the activity of students that make learning an accomplishment. Teachers who have never been asked to experience learning as discovery are unlikely to be able to carry this through in classrooms. Teachers who have experienced direct learning are more likely to appreciate its complexity and its power for other learners.

REFLECTION

Kenneth Zeichner and Daniel Liston (1987) contrast reflective action, which "entails the active, persistent, and careful consideration of any belief or supposed form of knowledge in light of the grounds that support it and the consequences to which it leads," with routine action, which "is guided primarily by tradition, external authority, and circumstance" (p. 24). The former describes thoughtful and intentional choice, while the later suggests reactive behavior, even victimization, in the face of received reality or circumstances. For Zeichner and Liston, "both teaching . . . and the surrounding contexts are viewed as problematic—that is, as value-governed selections from a larger universe of possibilities" (p. 25).

Donald Schön (1983) describes teachers engaged in reflective conversations with unique situations as "reflective practitioners." Reflective practitioners are people whose work relies less on positivistic science or technical rationality and more on reflective conversations—practical, experiential knowledge neither easily accessible to outsiders nor easily codified and technicized. Schön recasts intuition as a legitimate albeit undervalued form of knowledge, and he resists the tendency to force professional knowledge into a prescribed technical vocabulary.

Teaching involves moral, ethical, and social choice, dimensions that are difficult to teach or assess in straightforward ways, and are perhaps more suited to being achieved through reflection. Teaching also involves synthesizing all kinds of knowledge. Reflection is a process that can allow teachers to integrate personal, implicit knowledge with more objective knowledge, and along the way to render choices more controllable. Reflection is more than thinking, although thinking and thoughtfulness are essential to begin. Reflection is thinking rigorously, critically, and systematically about practices and problems of importance to further growth. Reflection is also linked to conduct, the ground from which it arises and to which it must flow. Reflection is a disciplined way of assessing situations, imagining a future different from today, and preparing to act.

CRITIQUE

Critique involves combating "the sense of ineffectuality and powerlessness that comes when persons feel themselves to be the victims of forces wholly beyond their control" (Greene, 1978, p. 64). It entails working closely with students to identify and overcome specific classroom problems. Changing classroom reality is part of critique, but it also might involve participating in society as citizens. Maxine Greene (1978) argues that democracy is inconceivable "in a society permeated by indifference, frozen in technological language, and rooted in inequities" (p. 71). She argues that teacher educators must be critical, "even political":

> Neither the teachers' colleges nor the schools can change the social order. Neither colleges nor schools can legislate democracy. But something can be done to empower some teachers-to-be to reflect upon their own life situations, to speak out in their own voices about the lacks that must be repaired, the possibilities to be acted upon in the name of what they deem decent, humane, and just . . . We can at least try to surpass what is insufficient and create conditions where persons of all ages can come together in conversation to choose themselves as outraged and destructive, when they have to, as authentic, passionate, and free. (p. 71)

Students of teaching can learn to oppose the banal and the petty, to protest both brutality and patronization in schools. Certainly they can oppose a watery curriculum that disengages and disempowers children. Students can learn to separate institutional constraints from human capacity, a history of injustice from the natural order of things. Students can come to the realization that schools are human constructions, and as such, humans can deconstruct or reconstruct them. Society is a human creation, after all, and it is subject to human re-creation.

If thinking involves enabling youngsters to ask their own questions and seek their own answers, then we need to move beyond the rather static, tight definition of teaching provided by Ravitch and Finn (1987): "explaining, questioning, coaching, and cajoling until children understand what adults want them to understand" (p. 204). We need to move from insight to decision, from understanding to action. To be aware of the social and moral universe we share, and aware too of what has yet to be achieved in terms of human possibility, is to be a teacher who is capable of being a critic and a public person. It is to be aware of one's work as more than inducting the young into a given world, of opening them to inquiry, imagination, critique, and invention. Teachers, like others, can join efforts to challenge what is unfair and unacceptable, and work to solve the overarching problems of our time. Teaching, goes beyond passing down the wisdom of the ages; it also is concerned with invention and transformation. Where tradition has been debilitating or oppressive, critical teaching includes opening students to ways to break the power that tradition exerts on people's lives. Critique invites teachers to be passionate, fervent people who are advocates for and allies of children and therefore somehow more naturally socially responsive, political, even activist.

COMMUNITY

Community involves practicing how to live and participate in the manifold of diverse ideas and people by combining the insights and the energies of many, and creating some dynamic consensus and harmony. Building a sense of community involves working with different publics, and developing a sense of fellowship and cooperation as a fundamental human need.

Community-building expands opportunities for sharing and overcoming problems, making productive connections, and acquiring deeper, more meaningful knowledge. While this can be valuable to students of all ages, it can be a particularly important factor in successfully overcoming obstacles and difficulties that teachers will surely encounter in practice. Community can be realized—if only partially and contingently—in a program where faculty exemplify or embody sharing, and practice a spirit of cooperation, caring, and compassion among themselves and with students.

*   *   *

While none of these areas of knowledge can be taught in a straight-forward, didactic manner, while none can be poured into the heads of inert students, each area can be valued, practiced, and examined. Public and private spaces can be created for reflection, for example. Students can be encouraged to work on autobiographical texts, and to view those texts as knotty and challenging. Students' concrete situations and ideas can be taken seriously, and an environment that provides opportunities for inquiry and critique can be pro-vided. Students can learn by doing, by being immersed in life in classrooms, and can work out ideas in dialogue with the problems they themselves pose.

Teacher educators might choose to direct the attention of stu-dents to areas often disregarded or denigrated and yet essential somehow in teacher education if teachers are not to be disabled and dehumanized before they begin. We may work toward giving stu-dents headaches, not because headaches are in themselves good, but because remaining open to growth and choice is an essential part of the full dimension of what good teaching is. Knowing one-self, knowing how to think, imagine, and make critical judgments, can help teachers choose themselves in the often frustrating and dreadful, always uncertain and ambiguous conditions of their teaching. Teachers might find relief for existing headaches, and they might even be moved to know more, to feel more, to touch children more, to reach out to each other more, to cry and to laugh more, to change the world more. Like Achebe's writer, the teacher might then be moved to bend toward the ethical and intellectual heart of the enterprise.

CHAPTER 16

About Teaching and Teachers

A MIDWIFE'S TALE

When we first met, Aña explained what her role would be in the upcoming labor and delivery of our baby. She talked about technical aspects of birth, routine interventions to anticipate, and some of the equipment and backup systems she would have on hand. Finally, she said this: "My skills and experiences can help you have the birth you want to have. The things I know can empower you."

I've thought a lot about that: "The things I know can empower you." How dramatically different this sounds from the widely accepted view of the all-knowing professional. From the traditional standpoint, professionals are the powerful ones, the ones with special knowledge and training that allows them to control and solve other people's problems. Teachers teach; lawyers litigate; doctors heal. The professionals are the active ones. They bring culture to the masses, remove tumors, and prescribe cures. Their clients receive ministrations and services passively, and become, then, educated, acquitted, or cured.

Communication with professionals is anemic, trivialized, and reduced to a tactical question of teaching style or bedside manner. It is rarely the heart and soul of a relationship that might unlock potential and power. Of course, there are doctors who acknowledge that the action of the body itself is the primary and essential healer, just as there are teachers who base their practice on an understanding that knowledge is acquired through an active process of construction and reconstruction. But it is interesting to consider how much of the language of professionalism is a top-down and inaccessible language of mystification and distance. Rarely is a professional person as clear as Aña was: "My job is to empower you, to help you take active control, to aid you in making the important choices."

Good teachers, like good midwives, empower others. Good teachers find ways to activate students, for they know that learning requires real engagement between subject and "object matter." Learning requires discovery and invention. Good teachers know when to hang back and be silent, when to watch and wonder at what is taking place all around them. They can push and they can pull when necessary—just like good midwives—but they know they are not always called upon to perform. Sometimes the performance is and must be elsewhere; sometimes the teacher can feel privileged just to be present at the drama happening nearby.

Midwives make themselves available to mothers and babies. They do not schedule a birth, and they cannot rely on some abstract timetable. Rather, midwives are "on call," and they assume that in most cases the baby will ring when ready. There are standards, to be sure, but they are flexible, participatory, built up in practice and never far from the action itself. Teachers also make themselves available to students. They, too, are on call, ready to seize the moment when a child is ready to learn or to grow.

In reference to a birth a midwife may say, "I witnessed a birth," "I attended a birth," or "I helped with a birth"; a midwife will not say, "I had another baby." Similarly, good teachers are comfortable enough to not confuse the central purpose or the major actors. They understand their own importance in the classroom, and they know it is their own vital relationship with children that is at the heart of the educational enterprise. And so, without belittling themselves, they are able to communicate to their students in a thousand ways, "You are of central importance here," "Your work is honored here," "Your discoveries and growth are respected here," and, finally, "You are the very reason we are here."

Does all this prescribe a passive teacher, a teacher who merely observes and approves? Not at all. A teacher who empowers is likewise made powerful. The teacher becomes an actor and an interactor. Like midwives carrying the black bag of professional tools, teachers bring their constantly developing experiences, their growing sense of themselves and their work, and their ever-widening knowledge of both content and craft to their efforts. Much of what they bring is learned on the job, for in teaching, as in midwifery, there is only so much you can talk about before immersion in the work itself initiates a never-ending process of training and growing.

Teachers accumulate experiences, skills, and techniques. They develop a repertoire that is complex, multilayered, and idiosyncratic.

Teachers, like midwives, must be improvisational and intuitive—no two births are exactly alike, just as no two classes, no two children, no two learning situations are the same in every detail. Teachers build a reflective practice, a praxis, that matures and develops and deepens. Good teachers seek the proper balance between content and children, between curriculum and students' real-life needs, abilities, concerns, feelings, dreams, and purposes.

Teachers and midwives are each part of an ancient profession, one that is currently undervalued and misrepresented in our society, but one that can trace its roots back through antiquity to the earliest stirrings of civilization—to healers, griots, gurus, and curanderas. In recent years our profession has struggled to base itself more firmly on modern scientific understandings and discoveries. Paradoxically, the more we understand about the science of teaching and learning, the more clearly we see that it is "embedded in a mystery." The more we hear from the biologist, the geneticist, and the physiologist, the more we see how incredible birth is. The more we hear from the educational researcher, the learning theorist, or the developmental psychologist, the more we stand in awe of the learner.

When our first child was born and he came slipping and bawling into our world, all of us there that morning were overcome with joy, relief, exhaustion, and hope as we cried and laughed and held onto one another. Aña was crying, too. How many births had she seen? Three hundred? Five hundred? And yet she yielded to the immensity and wonder, to the mystery, to the undiluted magic of the event. Ours was an intimate relationship—like the relationship with a very special teacher—that would be short-lived and could never achieve that kind of closeness or greatness again. Yet Aña gave the moment its due—she gave herself to its meaning in our lives. This was not just a birth, this was the birth of our first child. And it was the one and only miraculous birth for him, just as there would be only one amazing time when he first rode a bicycle, wrote his name, read a book, invented addition. Aña saw the moment as unique and maintained her awe, reverence, inspiration, and excitement—the very passion, as she once told me, that made her want to become a midwife in the first place.

I think there is a relationship between Aña's serious dedication to empowerment, her faith in and commitment to others, and her ability to maintain her values and humane perspective on her work. Because she opens herself to surprise and change, she avoids the dulling habits that become the prelude to burnout. Because she assumes a shared world of responsibility and personal meaning, she maintains perspective on accomplishment and fault. Meeting people on their own terms can be a powerful act of personal renewal.

PART IV

TEACHING

Inside every student—from kindergarten through graduate school—lurks an implicit question, often unformed and unconscious, rarely spoken. It's a simple question on its surface, but a question that bubbles with hidden and surprising meanings, always yeasty, unpredictable, potentially volcanic: Who in the world am I? The student looks inward at the self, and simultaneously faces outward, toward the expanding circles of context. Who *am* I, in the world?

Think of the college freshman, the first-year medical student, the thesis writer, the child anxiously looking at her mother on the first morning at day care. Who am I? What place is this? What will become of me here? What larger universe awaits me? What can I make of what I've been made?

The aware teacher knows that the question exists, that it perseveres. The wide-awake teacher looks for opportunities to prod the question, to awaken or agitate it, to pursue it across a range of boundaries, known as well as unknown. The challenge to the teacher—massive and dynamic—is to extend a sense in each student of both alternative and opportunity, to answer in an expansive way a corollary question: What in the world are my choices and my chances?

Each of us is better equipped to engage these questions if we work hard to understand the commitments we bring to the project of teaching. Some of these commitments may apply to all teachers and all teaching—a commitment to enlightenment, perhaps, a commitment to empowerment, although even this may be arguable—while others may be specific to this particular person at this unique time in this distinct place.

This section completes the circle, returning to the heart of the matter, to teaching itself. It is about deepest purposes and first principles. It rests on teaching's fundamental message: we can change ourselves and our world.

CHAPTER 17

Teaching as an Act of Hope

Before I stepped into my first classroom as a teacher, I thought teaching was mainly instruction, partly performing, certainly being in the front and at the center of classroom life. Later, amidst chaos and some pain, I learned that this is the least of it—teaching includes a more splendorous range of actions. Teaching is instructing, advising, counseling, organizing, assessing, guiding, goading, showing, managing, modeling, coaching, disciplining, prodding, preaching, persuading, proselytizing, listening, interacting, nursing, and inspiring. And a lot more.

Teachers must be experts and generalists, psychologists and cops, rabbis and priests, judges and gurus, and that's not all. When we characterize our work—even partially, even incompletely—straightforward images and one-dimensional definitions dissolve, and teaching becomes elusive, problematic, often impossibly opaque.

One thing becomes clear enough. Teaching as the direct delivery of some preplanned curriculum, teaching as the orderly and scripted conveyance of information, teaching as clerking, is simply a myth. Teaching is much larger and much more alive than that; it contains more pain and conflict, more joy and intelligence, more uncertainty and ambiguity. It requires more judgment and energy and intensity than, on some days, seems humanly possible. Teaching is spectacularly unlimited.

I find fragments of my own teaching everywhere, like pieces of a large quilt now filling my house, cluttering my mind. I remember Kelyn, a poor five-year-old African-American child I taught years ago. One day, Kelyn and I, with a half-dozen other kids on a trip from school, were playing the "I Spy" game. "I spy something red and white with the letters S-T-O-P on it," I said—my choices tended to be the easiest ones and, when too self-consciously geared toward "learning," the most boring as well. "Stop sign!" cried seven voices in unison.

A big brown truck pulled up to the stop sign opposite us. Darlene eagerly offered the next challenge: "I spy something brown."

Kelyn's eyes lit up and a broad smile crossed his face. He sat up as tall as he could, and with his right hand spread-fingered and flat on his chest, his left hand pulling excitedly on his cheek, shouted, "Hey! That's me! That's me!"

No one sensed anything peculiar or taboo or funny in Kelyn's response. After all, Darlene had asked for something brown, and Kelyn is brown. But for me there was something more—I was glad Kelyn had responded with unrestrained gusto. In that classroom we had spent a lot of energy on self-respect and affirmation and on exploring differences. Kelyn's father was active in the civil rights movement, and his parents were conscious of developing strong, positive self-esteem in their son. Kelyn was, I thought, reflecting and expressing some of that energy.

Kelyn and some of the other Black children were sometimes given to calling one another derogatory racial names, and I was painfully aware of hurt and rage. Here, for example, is a fragment of writing I found at that time, by 11-year-old Carolyn Jackson: *When I ride the train and sit next to a person of the opposite race I feel like a crow in a robin's nest/And I feel dirty.*

Carolyn expressed a powerful, perhaps dominant interpretation of what it means to be black in America: to be unwanted; to be "dirty"; to be a "a crow in a robin's nest." This was what I had been teaching against, and Kelyn made me feel like we had accomplished a small victory.

I remember another classroom, years later, and José La Luz, abused and neglected, a posturing 13-year-old wiseguy whose friends called him "Joey the Light." School failure fit José and followed him around like a shadow. Since he hated school and felt hurt and humiliated there, José made himself a one-man wrecking crew—the path to the principal's office was a deep rut he walked many times a day.

My struggle was to find something of value in José that we might build on, something he knew how to do, something he cared about or longed for, something that sparked some passion in him.

In March I saw a knot of kids skateboarding over and around some huge drainpipes at a construction site near school, and in the middle of it all, king of the mountain, was José La Luz. I asked José some days later if he could teach a minicourse on skateboarding to the class. He agreed. Soon we were subscribing to *Thrasher* magazine, organizing insignia design contests, and repairing skateboards on Friday mornings in a shop designed by José in one corner of the classroom. No one lived happily ever after—there was no sudden or perfect turnaround for José—but a moment of possibility, a glimmer of what could be for him, has remained in my mind.

Teaching is an act of hope for a better future. The rewards of teaching are neither ostentatious nor obvious—they are more often internal, invisible, and of the moment. They are deeper, more lasting, and less illusory than the cut of your clothes or the size of your home. The rewards are things like watching a youngster make a connection and come alive to a particular literacy, discipline, or way of thinking; seeing another child begin to care about something or someone in a way that he never cared about before; or observing a kid become a person of values because you treated her as a valuable person. There is a particularly powerful satisfaction in caring during a time of carelessness, of thinking for yourself in a time of thoughtlessness, of opening humanizing pathways for yourself and others, pathways that involve a quest. The reward of teaching is knowing that your life makes a difference.

I began teaching in 1965, and I have taught at every level, from preschool to graduate school: I have taught reading, math, and social studies, research methodology, and philosophy. I have cared for infants in a day care center and for adolescents in a residential home for delinquents. In every instance, there has been discovery and surprise, for me as much as for my students. Human relationships are just that way: surprising, idiosyncratic, unique, and marked by variety.

Over time, a basic understanding about teaching has emerged and become deeply etched into my own consciousness: Good teaching requires most of all a thoughtful, caring teacher committed to the lives of students. So simple and, in turn, so elegant. Like mothering or parenting, good teaching is not mostly a matter of specific techniques or styles, plans or actions. Like friendship, good teaching is not something that can be entirely scripted, preplanned, or prespecified. If a person is thoughtful, caring, and committed, mistakes will be made, but they will not be disastrous; on the other hand, if a person lacks commitment, compassion, or thought, outstanding technique and style will never really compensate. Teaching is primarily a matter of love. The rest is ornamentation.

CHAPTER 18

Teaching and the Web of Life

PROFESSIONAL OPTIONS AND FOLK ALTERNATIVES

> My practice is based on a view that each individual is a unique terri-
> tory to be mapped. This person is the subject of my study rather than
> a specific disease or particular symptom. Sometimes I'm not as useful
> as I'd like to be, not because I don't see the rash or hear the cough, but
> because I don't look deeply enough at the actual person before me, or
> I look in the wrong way. I need to see the whole person, and the whole
> context, and that can be very difficult indeed. But there are no stan-
> dard diagnoses, no uniform treatments, and no shortcuts. Each one is
> different.
>
> —Harriet Beinfield, personal communication

Harriet Beinfield and Efrem Korngold are practitioners of the
ancient healing arts of herbalism and acupuncture. Each was born
with healing in the blood: Efrem's father and Harriet's mother are
psychotherapists. Harriet's father is a surgeon, as were both of her
grandfathers. Both Harriet and Efrem grew up in a context of helping and healing. Taking care of people was a natural part of the webs
of their lives.

My own life story involves teaching. As the middle child in a
large and loving family, I had occasion to learn and to teach. Having
grown up in the 1950s and come of age in the turmoil of the 1960s,
teaching for me was a logical expression of commitment and caring,
a concrete connection to the imperfect but abiding human movement toward freedom and a better life.

I want to think about teaching, too, as an ancient art, and I want
to consider the vocational choice to teach and to heal. Untangling
some of the strands, reflecting on what we have been and what we
have become, we who live in a culture that glorifies the modern and
presumes to have conquered nature and the past may find our-

selves illuminated, perhaps even humbled, by the ancients. Sharing a dialogue of healing and teaching, doctors and teachers, we may find ourselves enriched and energized.

As Harriet talks of rashes and coughs, of heat and cold—"wind and fire" in her colorful, metaphorical language—of the idiosyncratic relationship between persons and symptoms that makes each cough different from every other in the diagnostic pattern, I think about teaching and about how teachers need to remember that each person is unique. As an early childhood teacher, for example, I have participated hundreds of times in the miracle of learning to read. I always tried to create a rich language experience, a healthy valuing of reading, a literate environment including a wealth of good literature in my classrooms. I read books, took dictation, made charts and labels, told stories, and found innumerable ways to encourage a sense of efficacy and authorship. And then, to be honest, I simply watched as child after child learned to read. Amazingly, each one was different. Zayd, for example, learned to read early by gulping down whole words and paragraphs; Malik memorized books on his way to reading; and Chesa played with sounds. One child knew the words to the entire Top 40 of any given week, and was delighted when I handed him a homemade book with the rock-and-roll lyrics typed out in large print; another child boldly accompanied paintings with elaborate hieroglyphics that moved toward recognizable letters and words only over time. Reading was confidently linked to discovery, and each moment was person- and situation-specific. It all seemed to me essentially mysterious.

Leo Tolstoy, the great Russian novelist, founded a school for the children of peasants on his estate a hundred years ago, and was deeply influenced by what he discovered about teaching and learning there. Tolstoy believed that each child learned to read in a singular way. He observed that what one child experienced as an obstacle to reading, another found to be an aid in the enterprise. He concluded that the best teachers did not attempt to discover the overarching perfect method for reading instruction, but rather had at their disposal the greatest possible number of methods, the ability to invent new methods as needed to fit particular situations, and an understanding, finally, that all methods are ultimately simplistic and one-sided. This is because teaching is not a method or even an accumulation of methods; rather, it is something of an art, a craft, a talent.

Tolstoy was not interested in a technique for teaching reading that in some statistical sense correlated with reading achievement scores. He was not thinking about averages or aggregates, grand theories or stereotypes with which to package what he did. Rather, Tolstoy's reflections highlighted the indefinite and profound process of teaching and learning. Tolstoy dignified teachers as interactive inventors of methods in an uncertain and changing universe.

The more familiar and dominant behaviorist view, on the other hand, is exemplified in this excerpt on reading instruction from *What Works* (1986), one of the U.S. Department of Education's dismal offerings in the current dark discussion of school reform:

> Children get a better start in reading if they are taught phonics. Learning phonics helps them to understand the relationship between letters and sounds and to "break the code" that links the words they hear with the words they see in print. (p. 21)

What Works embraces the scientific metaphor throughout, and here reduces reading to a technical or mechanical problem: an issue of decoding. The sense of real, breathing children, let alone the richness inherent in reading as a disposition of mind, is brushed aside in the interest of the general and the technical. The problems with *What Works* are its highlighting of technique, its seductive simplicity, and its closing of complexity.

Even the title betrays it. Here is something easy, modern, efficient, inexpensive, even painless. It works. I'm reminded that at the birth of the nuclear bomb, Robert Oppenheimer is reported to have said, "It works." When I was a child we all had our tonsils out; today pregnant women routinely have amniocentesis. People kill their crabgrass with the equivalent of Agent Orange, and our air conditioners, automobiles, shaving creams, and deodorants are literally killing the planet. But it is available. It works. Never mind the more jarring questions like: Why? So what? What for? With what effects? Abraham Maslow once said, "If the only tool you have is a hammer, you tend to treat everything as if it were a nail." No wonder we see learning disabilities everywhere we look today. We think we have that hammer.

Erik Erikson described every patient as a "universe of one"; he had in mind the specific problems and possibilities rooted in each psychological being. Harriet, with her "unique territory to be mapped," is concerned as well with a physical universe, the living homes of our intentions, the temples of our spirits. We would add, I think, a thoughtful universe and a moral universe. Seeing each person as a "universe of one" or a "unique territory to be mapped" frees us of the burden and the boredom of routine, as well as the multiple problems associated with treating other people like things. We are bothered by the implication of individualized solutions, because we know that the effectiveness of individual solutions depends so much on social, historical, and political realities. Conversely, the value and meaning of these big realities depends on authentic, individual lives. We are troubled, too, by proposing the same small changes that already have been subverted by larger social forces time and again. But we are also freed to build our community and our collectivity by engaging real people instead of organizing abstractions and shadows.

When we switch roles, when we become client to another's profession, the idea of being a "universe of one" is an exhilarating one. After all, I insist that I am more than my torn cartilage, more than my allergies, more than my grade point average or my political affiliation. When I am one down it becomes singularly important to be seen whole, to emerge from the crowd, to be treated as a person in need of help, perhaps, but in need of connection, too. I don't want cruelty, of course, but neither do I want condescension. I want understanding; I want solidarity. When I am one up, can I do any less? Consider the fatalities, small and large, that we scatter behind us when we fail to try. I suppose this explains why I sat on the operating table recently and engaged in a cheerful discussion about literature with the orthopedist who was about to insult my knee. I had no questions about his ability to cut and trim. I wasn't sure he cared. Behind our chitchat, I was fairly pleading with him to see me as whole, as I see myself.

We are challenged to ask how we know our patients and our students, those we would heal and teach. Who do we see when we look down at the treatment table or out across the classroom? Do we see a distant, objective, malleable mass living small, scripted lives? Or does our undeniable experience of choice and imagination extend to others? Do we see cancer or strep throat? Do we see inadequate family background? Do we see a behavior problem, a good girl, or (popularly today) a gifted and talented child or a learning disability?

These are important questions for teachers, awesome questions, because we begin to notice just what it is we hold in our hands. Children, yes, but something more: the dream and the hope to become someone. The whole truth about a person cannot be known objectively; it is not the result of standardized tests nor statistical measures nor the sum total of his or her data. A person can begin to be known only in relationship to context, to ground, to experience, to intention.

The world that teachers create speaks to the possibility of others inventing their own worlds. Our choice is the choice to shepherd other choices; our vocation is the vocation of vocations. That is a terrific responsibility, one that calls for humility and reverence—reverence for each child, humility in the face of each interaction. Teachers know they have found their own voices when they hear a chorus of other voices, of different voices, sometimes echoing, sometimes answering, eventually moving off in the distance. Only silence kills teachers. Yet it is precisely silence that the overly organized, technocratic system of education imposes. To insist on our voices—and to begin to link up with other voices—is to enter into risk and conflict. It is to move beyond method into the worlds of art and philosophy and politics.

Efrem contrasts the traditional and modern methods in healing:

> If I were to be run over by a bus, I would certainly want to be in New York City, close to a major hospital. There is no medicine in the world better able to intervene in crisis, none more successful in responding to life-threatening trauma and in bringing the full force of technology to bear in saving lives. The problem arises when machines, surgical procedures, drugs, and specialists become the model for medicine and for health. After all, it is the body that heals. We assist, but we don't control or dominate nature. (personal communication)

The physician is a helper, but it is the body itself that heals. Similarly, a teacher creates opportunities for experiences, environments for learning, and possibilities for growth and connection, but it is the child who learns. Healers and teachers are at their best when they enable others to get on with the business at hand.

Heroic intervention belongs to modern medicine. When I wrecked my cartilage I was glad for the microsurgery; when my friend ruptured a disk, modern miracle intervention was the best choice. In teaching, too, there are situations like these. The child who can't read because of a vision problem or a neurological disorder may well require a technical solution. But is that the equivalent of health? Is that education? The harm lies in overreliance and in splitting the person from the problem.

Harriet describes her feelings about her work this way: "It is more than what I do, it is who I am." Efrem adds, "It is in part a discovery of myself." Choosing healing, choosing teaching, is for healers and teachers a way of intensifying a sense of vitality. Teaching isn't something we do from nine to three; healing isn't something we peddle by the hour. It's at the core of ourselves. Teaching and healing merge—to heal is to teach, to restore wholeness; and to teach is to heal, to feed, and to nourish.

Donald Winnicott (1986) describes a healthy person as "taking responsibility for action or inaction" (p. 31). He includes a "tingling life" and the "magic of intimacy" in his sense of health (p. 31). Teaching is for many teachers a way of being healthy. Creativity in healing as in teaching is, in Winnicott's words, "the retention throughout life of something that belongs properly to the infant . . . the ability to create the world" (p. 40). Consciousness in teaching, as in healing, is more than critical thinking; it involves understanding context, biography, values, and vantage point; it involves the development of a fighting spirit, a willingness to act on what one knows, a linking of knowledge with feeling and with conduct.

Over 150 years ago, Chief Seattle, the great Native American leader, teacher, and healer, has been attributed by Indian oral history to have said, in an address to his people:

> This we know—the earth does not belong to us, we belong to the earth. All things are connected like the blood that unites one family. Whatever befalls the earth befalls the children of the earth. We did not weave the web of life; we are each merely a strand of it. Whatever we do to the web, we do also to ourselves.

This reminds us of our relational nature, our connectedness to one another and to a given world, our link to generations past and still to come, our contingency, our dazzling possibilities, and our responsibility to choose from the millions of possible paths. It reminds us, teachers and healers, of the ethical dimensions of our work, and calls us to a life of thoughtfulness, connection, and compassion. It counsels us to approach our tasks with humility and reverence, but also with a little toughness. To see our situations as they are, suspended in the web of life, is to be energized, to roll up our sleeves, and to wade into our work again with renewed purpose, rekindled passion.

CHAPTER 19

Work That Is Real

Here are snapshots of five different teachers in action:

Mr. Wilson, an elementary school teacher for over 20 years, tells his fifth graders on the first day of school that he has only three simple rules: "First, this is a learning community, and everyone needs to be safe here to work and to learn; no one is allowed to hurt anyone else, to hurt anyone's feelings, or to prevent anyone from doing the important work of our class." He explains that his rule applies to everyone—visitors, guests, and even to Mr. Wilson himself. He continues, "We'll discuss this a lot as the year goes on, and we'll discover how complicated it can be to figure out what's fair or what's right sometimes. For now, just keep it in mind, talk it over with each other if you'd like, and be sure to let me know if I do anything that might hurt someone's feelings."

The teacher has set an elevated tone by asking the children to consider something substantive and complex, noting that there are no simple, instantaneous answers, and there is nothing patronizing or punitive in it. "Second," he continues, "you can wear hats in this room, and third, you can chew gum—please don't make a mess with it." These two "rules" contradict school practice, and the announcement sends a wave of disbelief and energy through the students. There is a buzz of excitement, and a few laugh out loud—they are now together, a community of outlaws, resisting an unpopular, somewhat mindless school tradition, and Mr. Wilson is leading the conspiracy. Being part of this resistant community implicitly requires a higher level of strength and responsibility, and the fifth grade is already looking sharp.

*   *   *

Ms. Vaughn, a veteran middle school teacher, has discovered several dollars missing from the top drawer of her desk. She stands her eighth graders in a line and questions each child sharply about the missing money. "You're not moving until the thief confesses!" she shouts. The children stand for a long time, sullen and silent. She waits. When the bell rings ending the period, she accuses them angrily, "Some of you are robbers, and all of you are liars. You are the worst creatures I have ever taught." The children, eyes down, file out to their next class.

*   *   *

Mr. Smith has taught elementary school for five years, and currently teaches third grade. The science fair is fast approaching, and Mr. Smith has been instructed by the principal to develop a science project for his class. He has settled on dinosaurs, a classic standby, and while the children construct model dinosaurs with toothpicks and paste, Mr. Smith makes a poster that begins: "Hypothesis: What are the different names of the ancient dinosaurs?"

When the models are completed, Mr. Smith displays them on a table and announces, "This is a democracy, and so we'll vote for which ones to take down to the fair." One student suggests that they display them all. "No," Mr. Smith replies. "We don't want to embarrass ourselves." Another student notices that his model is missing from the table, and the teacher explains that "I've already weeded out the worst ones."

*   *   *

Ms. Cohen, a new kindergarten teacher, noting a school expectation that children develop an appreciation for different cultures and backgrounds, has taken a unique approach. For homework she has sent a note asking that families discuss and write up how each child came to have his or her name: Were you named after someone? Where does your name come from? What does it mean? The children bring back a breathtaking range of responses: Solomon's name is from the Bible, Aisha's from the Koran, Dylan's from popular culture, Malcolm's from the Black liberation movement, Lucia's from a grandmother in Cuba, and Veronica's from a comic strip. The names project opens a wide world of affirmation, vitality, and ongoing inquiry.

*   *   *

Ms. Ellis, an experienced elementary school teacher, has labeled every desk in her classroom with the words "left" and "right." "I can't teach them to

read," she explains, "if they don't know their left from their right." Ms.
Ellis proudly tells a visitor that "We're on page 307 of the math text—exactly where we're supposed to be according to board guidelines." Most of the
children are paying no attention, and the fact that virtually every child is
failing math is not her major concern. She is doing her job, delivering the
curriculum, and it is the children who are failing to do theirs. "I am a good
teacher," she declares, "but many of today's children simply cannot learn."

*   *   *

Anyone who spends time in schools could add hundreds, even
thousands, of other snapshots of teachers teaching: glimpses of
brilliance, cruelty, heroism, resistance, banality, capacity extended
and power abused. No single picture is ever entirely exemplary; no
snapshot ever reveals the whole of it. Yet each snapshot embodies
pieces of something larger, and looking at just these five, I wonder:
Should these teachers be empowered? Are they already powerful in
some hidden and some obvious ways? Would I want them running
our schools?

I recently attended an orientation for new teachers conducted
by a veteran elementary school principal. The administrator spoke
about his admiration for the idealism, the energy, and the fresh ideas
of his young staff. The tone was light and friendly, if unmistakably
patronizing—smiles and good feelings spread across the room. After a lengthy prelude of quips and compliments, the principal, without changing tone or facial expression, got down to business:

> I know you think you're going to change the world—and I
> admire you for it and I agree with it—but I don't want you to
> be too hard on yourselves. You think you can teach these kids
> to read, for example, and some will learn to read. But many
> come to us from homes where they never learn to listen.
> There's too much loud music, too much noise. For some of
> these kids, just getting them to listen would be a big job, an
> accomplishment. The main thing is not to be too hard on
> yourselves.

All the early praise of youth turns out to be an attack of some
substance. These teachers are being told that their aspirations and

their expectations are too high, that they are naive and foolish, that soon they can expect to grow out of it. They are being told that the failure to learn to read, for example, is the fault of the child and the family, not the responsibility of the school or the teacher.

Most teachers enter teaching with a sense of purpose and altruism. They attend colleges of education that muddy that purpose and communicate a large dose of disdain for that altruism. Afterwards, they enter workplaces that, too frequently, neither acknowledge, nurture, nor challenge them. And along the way, they meet a lot of people like this principal who patronize and mislead them. The structure of schooling combines with a defeatist and cynical school culture to render teachers silent, passive, and powerless in their own worlds.

All of this creates a teacher who is little more than a cog in a machine. Teachers become glorified clerks, mindlessly shuffling paper and carelessly moving through the workday. Bureaucratic thinking is not simply a problem at the central office; it impacts teachers and youngsters directly. Teachers come to think of themselves as interchangeable parts; they turn their attention to supervisors (whom they must please) and away from their students (who are expected, in turn, to mindlessly please them). In order to succeed, everyone must follow orders, march in step, become passive, and do the job.

If our larger purposes for children include the hope that they will develop a curious and probing disposition of mind, a compassionate and caring attitude, a critical and creative intelligence, and a willingness to participate in public life for the common good, how can mindless, uncaring, detached, alienated, and angry teachers achieve any of this?

What we find in schools, for children and for adults, runs counter to our avowed values and our larger purposes. Too often, we find disrespect in the lunchroom, dullness and conformity in the curriculum, bitterness and anger in the hallways. All the machinery of schooling—the bells, the intercom, the rows of desks, the endless testing of discrete skills—is a context that resists intelligence. Many kids, searching for what will allow them to succeed in school, reasonably conclude that obedience and dullness will bring rewards. And most teachers, having learned the "realities" (the limitations, the politics, the complexities) of life in schools, have learned to seek fulfillment elsewhere.

But would putting teachers in charge change any of this? Of course, teachers do run the schools now, in certain ways. Ask any principal, ask the public, or ask children and youth. Students know teachers directly, immediately. From the child's perspective, teachers are the potent embodiment of the entire school experience. A wider public knows teachers through the political clout of their unions and professional associations. Periodic strikes are a forceful reminder to the citizenry of teacher strength. And while principals describe their own power as contingent on a wide range of others—school boards, custodians, communities—they calculate their productivity and effectiveness in direct relation to teacher power. Teachers are at the center of the teaching–learning interactions; they are at the heart of the avowed purpose of the whole educational enterprise. Whatever they do or fail to do is, therefore, momentous.

The complexity of schools makes generalizability difficult. Combined with the imprecise and trendy application of language in our culture (and in education particularly), it can be difficult to know if a specific term is even referring to a similar universe of possibilities. A school is "restructured"; a classroom is "technologically advanced"; the curriculum is "revolutionized." But one has to be there to know the meaning of any of it.

When we talk of "empowerment," an educational buzzword that no one can seem to live without, we are on a slippery slope indeed. Are we referring to governance issues, economic issues, contractual issues, or pedagogical issues? Is "teacher empowerment" about the right to control the curriculum, revamp the school day, hire the principal, resist parental interference in textbook selection, discipline students, or protect contractual gains? It might be any of these or none of them.

Teachers appear, to the nonteacher world, to be people of authority, legal sanction, license, and influence. But teachers often experience themselves as powerless, abused, underpaid, and generally unappreciated. This paradox is difficult to unravel.

One focus of teacher power is the whole area of licensure and legal sanction. Every state compels teachers to fulfill specified educational requirements, to be citizens of solid character, to swear certain oaths or make particular affirmations, and, increasingly, to pass some form of standardized teacher test. When every requirement is fulfilled and every gate passed, the state consigns a license to teach;

it gives official authority and legal power to the teacher. This license is exclusive, and it endows the bearer with special privileges, responsibilities, and power.

Licensure is, of course, a contradictory kind of power. On the one hand, it provides teachers with privilege and authority: the privilege to be hired and the authority to work in the profession. On the other hand, in practice it can distort core aspects of teaching. For example, while the purpose of sanctioning a specific course of study may be to ensure a certain standard for teachers, this can, and often does, make the college or postgraduate experience exclusively a process of credentialing. Students of teaching become preoccupied with the utility of taking all the required courses for the certificate they want. In the process, they get their first serious taste of what is to come: they feel themselves made into objects within a bureaucracy. It becomes difficult, as a student, to experience oneself as an active subject in a world in need of help, perhaps even of repair. It is difficult, too, to stay alive to teaching as an intellectual and ethical activity.

As students pass through their courses of study, the original motivation that drove them to teach—love of children, perhaps, or a desire to share an important part of the world with others—begins to fade and is replaced with a sense of the functional and the technical. Students of teaching begin to submit to the given world of schools, to internalize the taken-for-granted, and not to think too much about it. Thus the power of licensure can also, in effect, undermine the power to teach.

A second center of teacher power is the union or professional association. Teachers' unions are organized as collective expressions of teacher power and a fact of life in U.S. schools. Over 80% of public school teachers are members of either the American Federation of Teachers (AFT—700,000 members) or the National Education Association (NEA—1,700,000 members), and more than 60% of teachers are covered by collective bargaining agreements. The AFT spearheaded the negotiated-conflict, trade-union approach to teaching; this has led to frequent strikes to improve wages and benefits. The NEA has been more consistently progressive on social issues such as racial justice and union democracy. Each organization has struggled to redefine itself in relation to changing school crises and realities. Both have moved in the direction of professionalizing teaching: the

AFT has championed career ladders and more learner-centered classrooms; the NEA has fought against arbitrary testing of teachers and the privatization of public schools. Each organization is somewhat defensive toward reform proposals, and each is evolving, however haltingly, from a collective bargaining, conflictual labor-management prototype toward a more professional policy–oriented stance. Together they have changed the face of U.S. education, and they remain a potent force from the state house to the school house.

But union power is contradictory. It has been enormously successful in gaining higher wages and benefits for teachers, and it has provided them with a vehicle for broader political participation. But union power has also generated several unintended consequences: it has identified teachers as an interest group engaged in special pleading (e.g., for school funding) that may be perceived to be against the public good (requiring ever-higher taxes). Union power has constrained teachers within a blue-collar framework with its exclusive focus on wages and benefits rather than on issues of curriculum, instruction, and evaluation. And union power has reinforced the problem of size. It has meant building big organizations necessary for the struggle with management, but these organizations have themselves become inflexible, impersonal, and bureaucratic in their own ways. Once again, teacher power proves to be problematic.

The most obvious and widely recognized venue for teacher power is the classroom itself. Central to the lore of teaching is the sense that once the classroom door is closed, teachers are autonomous and powerful. So while reform efforts generally focus on governance, administration, curricular change, and the like, teachers know that all of it depends on them. All reform must be filtered finally through their hearts and their minds; everything in classrooms lives or dies in their hands. While most often characterized as the base of the educational pyramid, teachers, in this sense, are at the peak of possibility and power.

But this power, too, is contradictory; it can divide and disconnect, isolating teachers from allies and colleagues. Since teacher rewards are mainly rooted in classrooms and teacher goals are primarily classroom-linked, teachers are less likely to seek or to offer help in relation to the content and conduct of their work. And since the structure of teaching develops a kind of radical individualism, teachers are typically conservative agents of continuity rather than dynamic agents of community change. Unfortunately, a range of advocated reforms—new math, cooperative learning, critical thinking—are premised on the notion that teachers should be interested in change and as such should be able to deliver what they currently neither understand nor practice. This is, of course, nonsense. So while the power to be autonomous can be invigorating, it can simultaneously cripple teachers in specific ways.

What, then, should schools look like? A school structured around what we know about teaching and learning would look dramatically different from today's schools. Typically schools are little factories: everything neat, ordered, and on schedule, or at least hoping to be so. Children are the products, moving passively along the assembly line, filling up with bits of subject matter and curriculum until they are inspected and certified to graduate to the next level. Teachers don't think much, don't question, don't wonder, don't care—they are the assembly-line workers. Never mind that between a quarter and a half of our kids fall off the line altogether, or that for those who keep moving along, the end of the line represents little opening of possibilities. Never mind that teachers are using only a fraction of their knowledge and abilities in these classrooms. The line itself has become the important thing, the line and the stuff being poured into the youngsters.

By contrast, schools that are powerful places for teachers to work recognize that people learn best when they are actively exploring, thinking, asking their own questions, and constructing knowledge through discovery; that people learn constantly and in a variety of styles and at a range of paces; that people learn when their emotional, psychological, physical, cultural, and cognitive needs are understood and addressed; and that people learn when they are nurtured but also challenged—when they are stimulated through encountering surprising new ideas and information that don't exactly fit their existing scheme of things.

In vital learning communities, children are actively engaged with a variety of concrete materials and primary sources, involved in purposeful work appropriate for their age. Teachers cannot be clerks in these settings, delivering a set of predetermined curriculum packages to passive consumers, but are coaches, guides, and co-learners. The first responsibility of teachers, then, is to see each student in as full and dynamic a way as possible, to discover the experiences, knowledge, preferences, aspirations, and know-how the children themselves bring with them to school.

Seeing the student as a center of energy in search of meaning is a complicated proposition, for there are always more ways to see, more things to know. Observation and recording are a way to begin, opening a process of investigation and affirmation. But it is understood that observations are always tentative, always in the service of the next teaching challenge, and always interactive—the observed, after all, are also people with their own intentions, needs, dreams, aspirations, and agendas. The student grows, the teacher learns, the situation changes, and seeing becomes an evolving challenge. As layers of mystification and obfuscation are peeled away, as the student becomes more fully present to the teacher, experiences and intelligences that were initially obscure become the ground upon which powerful teaching can be constructed.

Teachers create environments for learning, construct laboratories for discovery and surprise. In an early childhood classroom this might mean having a large block area, a comfortable reading corner, and an easel with red, yellow, and blue paints available. Working at the easel, a child might encounter orange and construct knowledge about primary and secondary colors upon making this dazzling discovery. Along with the color orange come confidence, self-esteem, curiosity, and a sense that knowledge is open-ended and that knowing is active. In contrast, a lecture and worksheet would be a rather tame alternative and would convey collateral lessons about knowledge as finite and knowing as passive.

In dynamic learning communities, teachers struggle to build bridges from the knowledge and experiences of youngsters to deeper and wider ways of knowing. Bridge building begins on one shore with the know-how and interests of the student and moves toward the far shore across experience, deeper ways of thinking and knowing. In this regard, it is worth transforming the old notion that "You can learn something from anything" into a deeper sense of relatedness and interactively: "You can learn *everything* from anything."

John Dewey (1916) argues that a big part of the art of teaching "lies in making the difficulty of new problems large enough to challenge thought, and small enough so that in addition to the confusion naturally attending the novel elements, there shall be luminous familiar spots from which helpful suggestions may spring" (p. 184). Children might connect issues in their own lives concerning society and the crowd, group identity, jealousy, and revenge to a deep encounter with *Romeo and Juliet*. It is all there, after all, in their lives *and* in Shakespeare. Teachers might find themselves covering less stuff but teaching everything more deeply.

Assessment, then, must reflect the whole child and is designed to illuminate strengths and interests as much as areas of need. Assessment is in the service of the next teaching question and must be broad and adaptive, rather than narrow and fixed. Teachers reject the obsession with a single, narrow assessment tool as inadequate to capture the complexity of human growth. Reinvented schools would develop a range of tools in order to achieve a rich, vital, and contextual portrait of learning.

Teachers have all kinds of power—some traditionally held, some won more recently—and yet none of it solves the problem of strengthening teachers or of creating learning communities in our schools. Existing power is too often irrelevant to the needs of teachers, outside of what they need. It does not speak to the imperative for schools to change, nor to the centrality of teachers in defining and building that process; neither does it address the possibility of a new kind of professionalism and the ways in which teachers could spearhead and benefit from breaking new ground. It ignores the nature of teaching and learning and the importance of teachers recognizing and wielding their real power in classrooms in new ways. Too much talk of teacher empowerment simply misses the point.

There are many more examples of failure than of success in the organized attempts to change or improve schools over the past several decades. The inconsistent role of teachers in generating reform is at the heart of much of the problem. As one educator notes with irony, the more things change, the more they stay the same. Not only are the unintended consequences of innovations often worse than the problems they were designed to fix, but existing regularities, the common sense of schooling, frequently prevent us from seeing the wider universe of possibilities. Mired in our own limited experiences, we are curtailed by crises in imagination.

We do, however, know by now what kinds of reform projects consistently flop. Failure is practically guaranteed:

- When curriculum packages are brought in from outside and fitted into existing structures and assumptions.
- When "in-services" are given to passive teachers in spite of their own priorities and felt needs.
- When reform is conceived as generic or one-size-fits-all.
- When classroom change is conceived and developed as "teacherproof."

These kinds of things promise easy change and painless improvement. Unfortunately, despite their consistent failure to deliver, they remain dominant in school improvement efforts.

The participants in successful school improvement efforts—teachers, parents, administrators, students—tend to be visible and accountable to one another. Successful change is not an imposed treatment, but an accomplishment achieved with all members of the school community acting as partners and allies. The improvement effort draws its power and energy from the needs and intentions of the people in the school community.

Successful school improvement projects are holistic; that is, they are not aimed at tinkering with bits and pieces of the school, but address intellectual and organizational issues, structural and cultural realities. Good ideas, curriculum guides, wonderful materials—all are of limited usefulness without, for example, rethinking the use of time, restructuring the roles of teachers and students, and reworking resources. Expanding roles and capacities, and challenging assumptions and the existing ethos are essential parts of successful change. It is, of course, easier to describe this process than to do it.

In successful school change, people actively define and then solve their own problems. Instead of reinforcing passivity and powerlessness, the change process itself develops agency and efficacy, the sense of oneself as an active participant able to create change. A guiding theme is that the people with the problems are also the people most needed to craft solutions. The process is important, and it leads to an action plan for all people in the school community.

What we know about successful school improvement argues decisively for an expanded role for teachers that moves them into the center of the change process—teacher empowerment. This is not something to be granted from "above" to teachers, but rather something teachers must themselves determine is necessary and right. Others may create the context for teacher empowerment, but teachers must initiate and exercise it themselves.

Teacher empowerment is already built into the teaching–learning interaction, the center of classroom life. Power characterizes certain relationships whether acknowledged or not, whether consciously exercised or not, whether overt or not. The power of teachers in classrooms is easy to illustrate. For example, in the vignettes at the beginning of this chapter, each teacher wields incredible power and yet each embodies a different sense of teaching, and power is therefore understood, exercised, and experienced differently. Ms. Ellis, whose failing math class was on the "right" page, is a clerk, delivering the curriculum to passive or resistant students. Mr. Smith is workmanlike in creating a science fair exhibition, attempting to shape the raw material that is before him. Ms. Vaughn is a guard, a disciplinarian, and an ineffective detective. Ms. Cohen and Mr. Wilson, on the other hand, demonstrate the power to tap into the strengths of children themselves, the power to empower.

Teacher empowerment will remain only a hypothetical proposition as long as it is conceived as a something granted from outside of teaching. Teacher power can never be simply mandated, legislated, or enforced; it must be taken by people who perceive the possibilities and are willing to overcome real obstacles, create unique alliances, and assume new responsibilities. Greater efficacy, vigor, and energy cannot be imposed on unwilling teachers. Teachers must claim their power by being willing to build and explore and extend it.

People outside of teaching cannot empower teachers, and yet this ingredient is essential to meaningful restructuring of schools and reforming of education. Teacher empowerment is a condition of reform, and it is teachers themselves who must choose to rethink and revive teaching.

Still, people outside of teaching can play a part. Teacher educators, for example, can structure programs that deemphasize the dominant focus on discrete skills and methods, choosing instead to create opportunities for students to work collectively, to actively construct knowledge about teaching, to resist the passifying, conforming traditions of teacher socialization. If they must teach methods, they can teach methods of creative insubordination. Educational researchers can move from doing research *on* teaching to conducting research *for* teaching, that is, choosing problems to research that are of collective interest to researchers, teachers, and students alike. They can promote action research, participatory research. And administrators, advocates, and funders can find ways to reward imagination and courage, to structure opportunities for teacher-initiated, collaborative efforts to take seed in schools and grow. They can remove the structural obstacles that currently debilitate teachers.

A fundamental goal of all teaching is the empowerment of others. All teachers at all times—regardless of philosophy, method, technique, or approach—want their students to become in some new way stronger, to have greater knowledge or capacity, to be more skilled or able or vigorous, to be able to survive or succeed in some new way. Empowerment is the heart and soul of teaching, and cannot be done well by the weak or the faint. There is no way for passive teachers to produce active students, for dull teachers to inspire bright students, for careless teachers to nurture caring students. Should teachers be empowered? Only if we want powerful students to emerge from our schools. Marge Piercy (1982) captures this in her poem "To Be of Use":

> The people I love the best
> jump into work head first
> without dallying in the shallows
> and swim off with sure strokes
> almost out of sight.
> They seem to become natives of
> that element,
> the black sleek heads of seals
> bounding like half-submerged
> balls.
> I love people who harness
> themselves,
> an ox to a heavy cart,
> who pull like water buffalo,
> with massive patience,
> who strain in the mud
> and the muck to move things
> forward, who do what has to
> be done, again and again.

I want to be with people who
submerge in the task, who go
into the fields to harvest
and work in a row and
pass the bags along,
who are not parlor generals
and field deserters
but move in a common rhythm
when the food must come in
or the fire be put out.
The work of the world is
common as mud.
Botched, it smears the hands,
crumbles to dust.
But the thing worth doing well
done has a shape that satisfies,
clean and evident.
Greek amphoras for wine or oil
Hopi vases that held corn,
are put in museums
but you know they were made
to be used.
The pitcher cries
for water to carry and
a person for work that is real.

Teaching, at its best, is just that: work that is real.

Conclusion

Every day of our lives is fleeting. "Swifter than a weaver's shuttle," Job laments, "my life is but a breath." Every moment is contingent, partial, and incomplete.

My attempt to name this dynamic and contested moment points to a time of deep crisis internationally and locally; a moment of shameless ascendant empire; an era of celebrity, acquisition, and propaganda, of domination overpowering accomplishment, education, and citizenship; a period of totalitarian impulse, of control and punishment, of criminal justice metaphors and practices pushing the great human enterprise of education aside. Naming the moment is itself a political act—an act of noticing, in the first place, and then of judgment and decision.

As I try to make sense of this moment, I notice contention and contradiction. Our society genuflects steadily to wealth and power and celebrity, yet simultaneously wishes to honor merit and fairness. We treasure equality and justice, but at the same time we seem mesmerized and speechless in the face of massive, growing gaps in wealth and access. Our country values peace on earth, good will toward all, yet has built the mightiest, most expensive war machine ever known, and has used it almost continuously.

We note discrepancies like these, spaces where our avowed and endorsed values came in conflict with some hard reality. The United States is large, of course, and it contains multitudes—it is full of life and possibilities, pulse, energy, buzz, hustle and bustle. It can stir our imaginations, call up our courage to live and to love. But vitality lives side-by-side with degradation, cherishing on top of alienation. We can choose to recover our humanity and our values, and fight to bring them more fully to life, or we can cover the conflict with public relations and sweet rhetoric, hoping it will go away. These essays are an expression of a lifetime spent arguing for the former.

Naming this moment closer to my focus here, I witness an organized and powerful attempt to crush a great progressive and democratic ideal—that every child and youth is entitled to a quality public education. This ideal has never been fully realized, but has been the democratic goal for centuries. But now it is in doubt. Powerful ideological forces have aligned themselves with specific, seemingly discreet policies in an attempt to undo the idea of a common public school available to all. For over 100 years we have struggled over who should be included in our sense of the public, what knowledge and experiences are of most value, how to access that knowledge and experience. Now the idea itself no longer seem secure; it no longer can be assumed.

The evidence of the abandonment is widespread and multi-layered. The accelerating obsession with a single and simple-minded centralized test that can do little more than rank students—at younger and younger ages—along a continuum of winners and losers, cuts at the heart of a democratic education, assaults any notion of a deep and rich curriculum, and undermines teaching. The energy and resources sucked into the testing business represent a demonstrable drain on commitments to put more qualified teachers in classrooms, to lower class and school size, to increase curriculum offerings and access to community learning resources, to build more modern schools, and on and on. The testing business cheats students, families, and teachers. It is a step backward for education.

"Zero Tolerance" policies, which have swept the country in the past decade—fueled in part by school shootings, and morphing quickly to embrace a host of issues beyond weapons—create conditions for the exclusion of large numbers of youth, especially poor and working-class kids, students of color, the children of certain immigrant groups, the marginal, the officially or traditionally despised. These policies are a cultural and political attack on inclusive, democratic schooling. Classrooms become sterile and one-dimensional places robbed of teachable moments. Every misbehavior warrants a trip to the office, teacher judgment and wisdom is curtailed, administrators become adjuncts to the police, and schools become narrow and prison-like. Common sense tells us, and study after study confirms the conclusion, that a truer, more effective approach to school safety involves reducing school size and class size. When

students are well-known by caring adults, when personal relationships and moral authority replaces bureaucracy and formal authority, schools are safer.

A range of school change strategies driven by a market model of
reform undermine the structures and the principles of public education. The vaunted marketplace has no heart and no soul—it cannot make judgments of value nor answer normative concerns. Yet,
the market always creates a class of winners and a larger class of losers. Success in the market is realized in profit: great wealth is generated through the labor of others. To impose a market metaphor
on a public enterprise like schooling is infused with disingenuous-
ness, beginning with the fact that no salable product is produced in
schools, and therefore money must come from a public fund. This
means the metaphor is false and on its head: public funds will still
be required, yet private interests will control and profit from them.

We can, of course, recognize and insist that the present moment—in spite of all we are told—is not the end of history. The
present moment is not a point of arrival. It is as dynamic, contested,
full of energy, and in-play as any moment ever was or ever will be.
History was not made in the 1960s or the 1990s or during the great
wars. History is being made right now. What we do and what we
don't do matters.

As Martin Luther King, Jr. was fond of saying: "The arc of the
moral universe is long, but it bends toward justice." This is an invitation to fight for something better.

References

Abbs, P. (1974). *Autobiography in education*. London: Gryphon.

Achebe, C. (1987). *Anthills of the savannah*. London: Heinemann.

Archambault, R. D. (Ed.). (1964). *John Dewey on education: Selected writings*. Chicago and London: University of Chicago Press.

Ayers, W. (1998). *Teaching for social justice: A democracy and education reader*. New York: Teachers College Press.

Ashton-Warner, S. (1963). *Teacher*. New York: Simon & Shuster.

Ashton-Warner, S. (1985). *Spinster*. New York: Simon & Shuster. (Original work published 1958)

Baldwin, J. (1963, December 21). A talk with teachers. *Saturday Review*.

Baldwin, J. (1995). My dungeon shook. In *The fire next time*. New York: Modern Library.

Bell, D. (1992). *Faces at the bottom of the well*. New York: Basic Books.

Bellah, R. et al. (1985). *Habits of the heart: Individualism and commitment in American life*. Berkeley: University of California Press.

Dewey, J. (1916). *Democracy and education: An introduction to the philosophy of education*. New York: MacMillian.

Duckworth, E. (1987). *"The having of wonderful ideas" and other essays on teaching and learning* (2nd Ed.). New York: Teachers College Press. (Original work published 1978)

Gaines, E. (1993). *A lesson before dying*. New York: Alfred A. Knopf.

Gates, H. L., Jr. (1995). Why now? In S. Fraser (Ed.), *The bell curve wars*. New York: Basic Books.

Gatto, J. T. (1992). *Dumbing us down: The hidden curriculum of compulsory schooling*. Philadelphia: New Society Publishers.

Goodlad, J. (1988). *Educational renewal: Better teachers, better schools*. San Francisco: Jossey-Bass.

Greene, M. (1978). *Landscapes of learning*. New York: Teachers College Press.

Grumet, M. (1978). Curriculum as theatre: Merely players. *Curriculum Inquiry, 8*(1), 37–64.

Haberman, M. (1995). *Star teachers of children in poverty*. Bloomington, IN: Kappa Delta Pi.

Holt, J. C. (1989). *Learning all the time*. Reading, MA: Addison-Wesley.

hooks, b. (1994). *Teaching to transgress.* New York: Routledge.

Hughes, L. (1994). *Collected poems.* New York: Alfred A. Knopf.

Jelloun, T. B. (1999). *Racism explained to my daughter.* New York: The New Press.

Kidder, T. (1989). *Among schoolchildren.* Boston: Houghton Mifflin.

Kohl, H. (1988). *36 children.* Philadelphia: Open University Press. (Original work published 1967)

Kohl, H. (1984). *Growing minds: On becoming a teacher.* New York: Harper & Row.

Kozol, J. (1991). *Savage inequalities: Children in America's schools.* New York: Crown.

Kuhn, T. (1970). *The structure of scientific revolutions.* Chicago and London: University of Chicago Press.

Lopate, P. (1975). *Being with children.* Garden City, NY: Doubleday.

Lortie, D. C. (1975). *Schoolteacher: A sociological study* (2nd Ed.). Chicago: University of Chicago Press.

Maalouf, A. (1994). *Samarkand.* London: Abacus.

Malcolm, J. (1990). *The journalist and the murderer.* New York: Vintage.

Malouf, D. (1993). *Remembering Babylon.* New York: Pantheon Books.

Maslow, A. Available at http://www.humansciences.net.an/news/MaslowsHierarchy.htm

Means, B., & Olson, K. (1995). Leadership for technology implementations. In *Technology's role in education reform: Findings from a national study of innovating schools.* Washington DC: Office of Educational Research and Improvement, U.S. Department of Education.

Meier, D. (1995). *The power of their ideas.* Boston: Beacon Press.

Morrison, T. (1993). *Acceptance speech to the Swedish Academy on the occasion of the awarding of the Nobel Prize in literature.* New York: Alfred A. Knopf.

Morrison, T. (2000). *Beloved.* New York: Penguin.

Neruda, P. (1975). The poet's obligation. In *Fully empowered* (A. Reid, trans.). New York : Farrar, Straus and Giroux.

Olson, L. (1988, November 2). The "restructuring" puzzle. *Education Week, VIII*(9), 7–11.

Piercy, M. (1982). *Circles on the water.* New York: Alfred A. Knopf.

Ravitch, D., & Finn, C. E. (1987). *What do our 17-year-olds know?: A report on the first national assessment of history and literature.* New York: Harper and Row.

Rose, M. (1989). *Lives on the boundary: The struggles and achievements of America's underprepared.* New York: Free Press.

Sandburg, C., & Steichen, E. (2002). *The family of man.* New York: The Museum of Modern Art.

Schön, D. (1983). *The reflective practitioner.* New York: Basic Books.

Seattle, Chief. Available at http:/www.barefootsworld.net/seattle/html.

Sykes, G. (1987). Some benefits of creating macro-contexts for science instruction: Initial findings. *Journal of Research in Science Teaching, 24,* 417–435.

Szymborska, W. (1997). A word on statistics. *Atlantic Monthly, 279*(5), 68.

U.S. Department of Education. (1986). *What works: A practical guide for parents and teachers.* Washington, DC: U.S. Department of Education, Office of Educational Research and Improvement.

Walker, A. (1983). *In search of our mothers' gardens: Womanist prose.* New York: Harcourt.

Wiggington, E. (1988). *Sometimes a shining moment: The Foxfire experience.* Garden City, NY: Anchor Press/Doubleday.

Winnicott, D. W. (1986). *Home is where we start from: Essays by a psychoanalyst.* New York/London: W.W. Norton; Hammondsworth: Penguin.

Wood, G. (1992). *Schools that work: America's most innovative public education programs.* New York: Dutton.

Zeichner, K., & Liston, D. (1987). Critical pedagogy and teacher education. *Journal of Education, 169*(3), 117–137.

Index

About the Author

William Ayers began teaching in 1965 in an experimental free school associated with the civil rights movement. He has been involved in community and adult education, prison education, and a variety of school reform projects and movements. He has taught preschool through graduate school, has lived in a residential home for "delinquent" youngsters, and has founded and directed three different alternative schools. His own children have been a major source for thinking and rethinking issues of teaching and learning. He is author of *The Good Preschool Teacher* (Teachers College Press, 1989), and *To Teach: The Journey of a Teacher, Second Edition* (Teachers College Press, 2001). Currently a Distinguished Professor of Education at the University of Illinois at Chicago, he lives with Bernardine Dohrn in Hyde Park, Chicago.